Bravely Fought the Queen

A Play in Three Acts
by Mahesh Dattani

This edition of *Bravely Fought the Queen* first published in 2003 by:
Border Crossings Ltd.
13, Bankside
Enfield
EN2 8BN

Tel/Fax: +44 (0) 20 8361 2308
email: books@bordercrossings.org.uk
website: www.bordercrossings.org.uk

2nd edition 2008

A catalogue record for this book is available from the British Library.

ISBN 978-1-904718-03-1

Printed by Kent Print Management

Introduction to Mahesh Dattani's *Bravely Fought the Queen*
by John McRae

Like all Mahesh Dattani's plays, *Bravely Fought the Queen* is engaged in the exploration of space. The inside spaces of the characters' souls and emotions, the outside spaces of rooms, offices and houses, the spaces between partners, friends, insiders and outsiders, and of course the theatrical space between players and audience – all of these are part of his space programme.

The indeterminacy of these spaces is the dynamic of the conflicts of the play: every character is in search of space to share or space to conquer. In the Border Crossings production the "home" space was easily crossed, into an indeterminate stage space, and the all-seeing television reshaped and redefined all the spaces the audience could see.

Michael Walling, in his introduction to this play for the Penguin India *Collected Plays* edition (2000), wrote perceptively, "his plays fuse the physical and spatial awareness of the Indian theatre with the textual rigour of western models like Ibsen and Tennessee Williams. It's a potent combination, which shocks and disturbs through its accuracy, and its ability to approach a subject from multiple perspectives."

These multiple perspectives are like the multiple spaces on the stage, and the multiple needs, wants, desires and ambitions of the characters. Of these it is perhaps Lalitha who is the most obvious: pushy, intrusive, but at the same time naïve and innocent, she is the most straightforward in making her way to getting more and more of what she wants. But only the audience can actually see the deeper needs and wants of all the characters, only they are privy to the great secrets. Nitin's final speech strips away the deepest secret that he cannot express, even to Alka: the final words "those powerful arms" resonate long after the final curtain. They are the simple physical expression of so many of the deepest needs of practically every character, female as well as male, the physical embrace that cannot be asked for, the simple human understanding that has been stunted, truncated like the bonsai, knowledge that cannot be fully understood until and unless it is shared with the audience.

The female characters seem on the surface to have the best of this play – it is full of good meaty roles for actresses. Beside them the men might seem to be symbols or stereotypes, especially Kanhaiya, with the dark skin and strong arms. But Dattani is on record as saying that the biggest stereotypes are "men" and "women". And in all his plays he is engaged in redefining men and women and their roles in modern society, not only in India.

This play is full of historical and cultural allusions. The very title comes from a traditional Hindi text "we learnt in school … but had to translate it in English as an exercise." With its refrain of "so bravely fought the manly queen" it is right up to date in its questioning of female and male roles in society, and Dattani's slight change to that quotation is indicative: what used to be just an exercise in translation is now an exercise in human understanding.

To examine Indian culture, Mahesh Dattani uses English. No apology is needed, nor any explanation. There is no elitism here, none of the snobbery which attaches to some Indian writing in English. I have frequently heard him be asked, "Why don't you use your own language?" He always smiles benignly and responds, "I do." Born in Gujarat, brought up in Bangalore, he is fluent in at least three languages, but chooses to write his plays in English. His early reading in Samuel French's editions of plays in

English borrowed from the British Council Library in Bangalore brought him into contact with playwrights from Ibsen (who among us could read him in the original Norwegian?) to Neil Simon, from Shaw and Maugham to Alan Ayckbourn. From them he learned how to construct a play. From Indian culture he learned how to move out of the enclosed space of the drawing room or kitchen and into the multiple layers of space that India teaches us to live in. India is full of space invaders: no space is sacrosanct, except perhaps some of the deepest inner space of the individual. This is space exploration of a crowded society, and there is at the same time in *Bravely Fought the Queen*, as so often in Dattani's plays, a sense of claustrophobia, a clamouring to break out of enclosed spaces, and the sense of another vast space in there or out there somewhere.

That such struggles can be funny as well as deeply moving is testament to Mahesh Dattani's immense sympathy with his characters – the pushy Lalitha is both hilarious and touching in her concern for her bonsai; Baa is very moving in her wandering and wondering; the men, with their barely contained violence and need for a shoulder to cry on, can be frustrating and can seem weak, but they are having to negotiate with centuries of imposed roles which suit them less well than the 'stereotypes' the women are allowed to play. Kanhaiya, with his dark skin and strong arms can be seen as Krishna, who is literally 'the dark-skinned one.' The seeker is a woman and the goal is Krishna. It is not so much about the man/woman battle as about the battle to deal with the roles one is allotted and the roles one wants to play. Sexuality or longing for the divine union is a female role. Krishna as a man is everywhere: one man for every female longing. One longing for every man? Is Nitin's longing not the same as the longing of any of the female characters?

The manly queen and the queenly man – there is, for us, an obvious play on words here. Alka's "oh, let me play the queen please" is the author's favourite single line in the play. Who is to play the queen? The question is universal. As I said in my introduction to *Final Solutions and other plays* (1994), "his plays speak across linguistic and cultural divides – they will work equally effectively in England or Italy, India or Brazil. Yet they need never be transposed out of their clearly Indian settings. As Chekhov remains resolutely Russian while his plays speak universally, so Dattani has created images, characters, and plots which reverberate with the reality of India today. They use Indian mythology, Indian traditions, Indian dance, Indian English, and Indian social problems – yet speak of themes which touch any audience: the search for individual identity inside and outside the family; the need for happiness, love, sexual fulfilment, security; the loneliness and emptiness of superficially successful lives; belonging and not belonging; the pain and pathos of keeping up appearances." Looking back at that paragraph it is astonishing to see just how many of these themes are right here in *Bravely Fought the Queen.*

This is India today, and the world today. It is important that it is not "post-colonial" India, or "the Empire writes back," as fashionable academic jargon might have it. Mahesh Dattani has said to me explicitly, "it is writing, and it is no longer an empire. So that phrase is 'politically incorrect'."

He himself is light-hearted about how critics and academics "may actually even succeed in finding all that stuff in my lil ol play." He carries his achievements lightly, but takes his work immensely seriously. It is written for audiences. The three Acts of *Bravely Fought the Queen* are headed **"The Women", "The Men"** and **"Free for All."** That is a breakdown of role divisions that every audience can respond to.

John McRae

May 2003

John McRae is Special Professor of Language in Literature Studies at the University of Nottingham

Bravely Fought the Queen was first performed at Sophia Bhabha Hall, Bombay, on 2 August, 1991. The cast was as follows:

DOLLY TRIVEDI	Veena Sajnani
LALITHA	Tara Ramaseshan
ALKA TRIVEDI	Sandya Kutappa
BAA	Munira Sen
JITEN TRIVEDI	Chippy Gangjee
NITIN TRIVEDI	Ashish Sen
SRIDHAR	Salmin Sheriff
Director	Mahesh Dattani
Lighting	Paresh Kumar
Stage Managers	Kumuda Rao Nanda Kishore

It was first performed in the UK at Leicester Haymarket Studio on 3 April, 1996. The cast was as follows:

DOLLY TRIVEDI	Siddiqua Akhtar
LALITHA	Suchitra Malik
ALKA TRIVEDI	Harvey Virdi
BAA	Adlyn Ross
JITEN TRIVEDI	Harmage Singh Kalirai
NITIN TRIVEDI	Dhirendra
SRIDHAR	Pravesh Kumar
Directors	Mahesh Dattani Michael Walling
Lighting	Stephen Barnett
Stage Manager	Jennie Stogdon

CHARACTERS
(in order of appearance)

DOLLY TRIVEDI, mid thirties
LALITHA, early twenties
ALKA TRIVEDI, early thirties, Dolly's sister
BAA, late sixties, paralysed, Jiten and Nitin's mother
JITEN TRIVEDI, forty, violent, Dolly's husband
NITIN TRIVEDI, late thirties, Jiten's brother, Alka's husband
SRIDHAR, mid twenties, Lalitha's husband

The action takes place in the residence of Jiten and Dolly Trivedi in Acts One and Three, and in the offices of Jiten and Nitin Trivedi in Act Two.

Time: the present.

ACT 1

The Women

(The living room of Dolly and Jiten Trivedi, in a posh suburb of Bangalore. The decor is expensive, perhaps tasteful, but badly maintained. Upstage centre is dominated by a well-stocked bar. On a higher level is the bedroom of Jiten and Niten's mother, referred to as Baa. She is bedridden and is visible through the screen wall when it is back-lit. A staircase is visible along with a small landing which leads to both Baa's bedroom and Dolly's bedroom off-stage. Upstage left is a largish window overlooking the front of the house. Next to it is a stereo system – music can be heard. It is a thumri sung by Naina Devi. Downstage left, exit to the kitchen and downstage right is the main door of the house.
Dolly is seated on the sofa, wearing a dressing gown, lost in the thumri, perhaps humming along with it. She is aimlessly filing her nails. She has a mud mask on and her hair is in clips. After a while, the doorbell rings. She gets up and opens the door to Lalitha, who is carrying a large bag and a shopping bag.)

LALITHA: Hello.

DOLLY: *(puzzled.)* Oh, hello? *(Short pause.)*

LALITHA: How are you?

DOLLY: *(still groping.)* Fine? *(Pause.)*

LALITHA: *(bursts out.)* Your husband asked me to come and meet you!

DOLLY: Oh! You mean tonight? *(Lalitha nods.)* Come in. Come in.

LALITHA: *(enters.)* I'm sorry if you didn't expect me.

DOLLY: Oh, I did. Not tonight, though. There must be some mix up. Er – sit down.

LALITHA: *(sits down.)* Well, I'm glad you are at home, considering–

DOLLY: *(turns off the stereo.)* Well, I'm not going to be home very long.

LALITHA: I was told you would be here – of course, you're here but…

DOLLY: As you can see, I was getting ready. *(Pats her mask.)* My mask is almost dry.

LALITHA: I lie down under the ceiling fan.

DOLLY: Huh?

LALITHA: When I have my mask on. It dries faster.

DOLLY: Oh, I see.

LALITHA: Then I can do my meditation in shavasana at the same time. Once the neighbour's boy peeped through our window and saw me lying flat on my back in the middle of the room. He thought I was dead or dying or something. He called the watchman. When I opened the door for them, they both thought I was a ghost, what with all that mud on my face and egg on my hair. *(Laughs. No response from Dolly.)*

DOLLY: I'm sorry. I wanted to laugh but I was afraid.

LALITHA: Afraid?

DOLLY: Afraid I would crack my mask.

LALITHA: Oh, yes. It happens to me all the time. I–

DOLLY: Look, I know we have met but I have an awful memory...

LALITHA: Oh, that's okay, I understand. You must be meeting a lot of people at parties. I'm Lalitha.

DOLLY: I did remember your name, Lalitha–

LALITHA: *(smiling.)* It's okay even if you didn't.

DOLLY: No, no. I did. What I was trying to remember was – whose wife are you? I know we met at the office party last month so you must be somebody's wife. *(Pause.)* What I mean is your husband – I know – is working for my husband. Jiten did mention that Lalitha will be coming and she happens to be so-and-so's wife. Which is what I have forgotten. Whose wife are you?

LALITHA: I get what you mean. Well, I'm Sridhar's wife.

DOLLY: *(feigning recognition.)* Oh! You are Sridhar's wife! Of course!

LALITHA: You do remember him, don't you?

DOLLY: *(meekly.)* No.

LALITHA: He handles the ReVaTee account.

DOLLY: I'm afraid I don't know much about my husband's work.

LALITHA: They are their biggest clients. Sridhar handles them. Your husband and your brother-in-law call him ReVaTee Sridhar because there are so many Sridhars in the office. All my husband does at home is talk about his work.

DOLLY: Look, it's been really nice meeting you again, Lalitha, but I must get dressed. Jiten will be here soon to pick me up.

LALITHA: Oh no!

DOLLY: Is anything wrong?

LALITHA: I'm sorry but I can't leave.

DOLLY: *(a little warily.)* You can't leave? *(Lalitha shakes her head.)* Why not?

LALITHA: Where do I go?

DOLLY: Home?

LALITHA: It's too far. I can't go on my own.

DOLLY: Why don't you call your husband and ask him to pick you up?

LALITHA: He just dropped me here!

DOLLY: Where did he go?

LALITHA: To the office!

DOLLY: That's where my husband is!

LALITHA: That's why he's gone there!

DOLLY: *(not quite understanding.)* After dropping you here? He came all the way to Koramangala to drop you here and then went back to Grant Road?

LALITHA: Because Mr Trivedi asked him to.

DOLLY: My brother-in-law?

LALITHA: No, your husband. They are meeting there to discuss important work.

DOLLY: Well, if they are there, then it's simple. *(Moves to the phone.)* I'll just call the office and sort it out. *(Dials.)*

LALITHA: Did Mr Trivedi at least tell you why we were meeting?

DOLLY: Engaged. *(Dials again.)* Hmm? To be frank with you, I had even forgotten all about it.

LALITHA: We are supposed to discuss the masked ball.

DOLLY: Engaged. *(Hangs up.)* Oh, well. Your husband will find out.

LALITHA: What?

DOLLY: As soon as he gets to the office, he will realize that there has been a mix-up and that Jiten and Nitin are heading here. So, he will come back as well and pick you up. We are going to the Kapoors. All four of us. Jitu said it was important we all go.

LALITHA: Oh. In that case, Sridhar must have got the dates mixed up. He doesn't usually. Well, I'm sorry but I'll have to wait till he comes back.

DOLLY: That's all right.

LALITHA: It may take some time. He may not have petrol in his motorbike. He may have stopped to fill some.

DOLLY: It's all right.

LALITHA: If we were living close by, I would have taken an autorickshaw home, but–

DOLLY: There's no problem!

LALITHA: But we live in RT Nagar. The other end of the world. Sridhar thinks it is unsafe for women to move about alone at night. I hate to admit it, but he's right. *(Sighs.)* They should have women auto drivers. You might still lose your jewellery, but at least you won't get raped.

DOLLY: *(picks up her nail file.)* Wait as long as you want. *(Sits down and starts filing her nails.)*

LALITHA: *(opens her bag and looks at Dolly.)* We might as well discuss it.

DOLLY: What?

LALITHA: The ball. Mr Trivedi did tell you why we were meeting?

DOLLY: He did say… I think I've forgotten.

LALITHA: *(takes out a book or list.)* Sridhar came up with this fabulous idea – *(Giggling.)* – I guess I should be more modest about my husband's work but, anyway – Sridhar had this fabulous idea of a masked ball to launch ReVaTee. We invite all the big shots and the press, and at midnight we reveal the model for our ad campaign. The best part about the ball is everyone will be in costumes! And will have masks on!

DOLLY: Wonderful. What is ReVaTee?

LALITHA: It's a new range of colour-coordinated nightwear and underwear for women. Very exclusive stuff. Now this is extremely confidential – we haven't as yet bagged the account. They are doing what is called speculative campaigning.

DOLLY: And what are we supposed to be discussing tonight?

LALITHA: Oh, sorry. Here's the list of invitees. Mr Trivedi said you know most of the Tablers' wives. *(Hands over the list to Dolly.)* You are supposed to suggest costumes for all of them.

DOLLY: Why me?

LALITHA: Well, he did say you had some experience in tailoring. *(Pause.)* I guess it's nice to know a bit of this and that.

DOLLY: *(gives Lalitha the list, quietly.)* Take this. I am not in a mood to discuss this. *(Lalitha takes back the list from her and nervously puts it back in her bag.)* I am going out. Out. And I need to relax before I dress up. You understand?

LALITHA: *(intimidated.)* Yes. Of course. *(Pause.)*

DOLLY: What else did he tell you? About me.

LALITHA: Oh, nothing! Nothing at all!

DOLLY: Good. *(Pause. Dolly continues to file her nails.)*

LALITHA: What a lovely house!

DOLLY: Yes. *(Pause.)* It's the same as theirs.

LALITHA: What?

DOLLY: The house. We have twin houses.

LALITHA: Oh yes, I know. It's a fantastic idea. Really cute.

DOLLY: They built them together. They got an architect from Bombay to design them.

LALITHA: He's done a great job.

DOLLY: Twin houses. Right in the middle of nowhere.

LALITHA: *(nods in agreement.)* It is soo inconvenient for us, I can't tell you! Mind you, once we are there it looks as busy as anything. But – over here – you don't even have neighbours yet. Don't you feel, you know, isolated?

DOLLY: *(laughs hard, then stops.)* Oh! I've cracked my mask. *(Pats her mask.)* Isolated. Yes. But they were adamant. They wanted their huge beautiful houses. Twin houses. Side by side. One for each brother. And two sisters! One for each brother!

LALITHA: *(laughing.)* I think that's really...

DOLLY: Really what?

LALITHA: *(seriously.)* I think it's really fantastic that your sister lives right next door to you. Mine's in the States.

DOLLY: Yes. *(With a slight edge.)* Fantastic.

LALITHA: *(senses she has hit upon a touchy subject.)* Er... how many rooms?

DOLLY: Three bedrooms. Two upstairs and one down. Daksha prefers the downstairs one.

LALITHA: Daksha?

DOLLY: *(looks at her.)* I don't suppose Jiten mentioned our daughter to you?

LALITHA: No. But I haven't spoken to him very much.

DOLLY: *(to herself.)* He doesn't mention Daksha, but he mentions my tailoring.

LALITHA: Hmm? She must be in school.

DOLLY: Yes. Yes, she is in school. She goes to – let me see *(she closes her eyes, thinking desperately.)* – Ooty. Yes. She goes to a school in Ooty.

LALITHA: Which one? Blue Mountain? My cousin's son is studying there!

DOLLY: *(stares at Lalitha.)* No. Not Blue Mountain. The other one. *(Resumes filing her nails.)* Then there's Baa. My mother-in-law. We had to put her in the upstairs room because of Daksha. Baa had a stroke.

LALITHA: Oh! How terrible! How is she now?

DOLLY: She's alive. *(Rises suddenly.)* Well, the kitchen is here. There's a back door which leads to the servants' quarters. The watchman's and...

LALITHA: And?

DOLLY: The cook's.

LALITHA: Oh! An old trusted family servant.

DOLLY: Yes. Old and permanent. *(Crossing to Lalitha.)* The trusted old family cook has gone on a holiday.

LALITHA: Oh. You must be missing him.

DOLLY: No. Not at all. He has left a replacement. Till he comes back.

LALITHA: Very thoughtful of him. *(Pause. She has had enough.)* Look, I'm positive your husband said tonight. We have to discuss the ball. Otherwise he will take it out on Sridhar. Can I call the office? If he has got there I can ask him to come right back.

DOLLY: My mask is all cracked. Yes, do that. Excuse me, I have to wash and get ready.

LALITHA: Oh sure. I'll just use your phone if you–

DOLLY: Please – please go ahead. *(Exits to her bedroom.)*

LALITHA: *(dials.)* Hello? It's me. Ya. Thank God you've reached. It looks like you've got the dates mixed up... No, she wasn't expecting me... No, it's not just that. She tells me they are going out somewhere... *(Impatiently.)* 'They' means she and her husband, her sister and her husband. I know they are there but she is so sure of it... Oh... Oh! Then she has got her dates mixed up... Well, she is getting dressed now... Look. What do you want me to do? I can't discuss the ball with her, she doesn't want to! Wait for an hour? But what if she wants to go out? ... How are you so sure? ... Oh... Oh, I see... Okay. If you say so. I could go over to her sister's house if she wants to be left alone. So if I'm not here, I'll be next door... Don't be late. Bye. *(Lalitha hangs up and hesitantly looks towards the stairway. Then she sits down. She is ill at ease. Suddenly a loud bell rings. She jumps up. An old woman's voice is heard.)*

BAA: *(off.)* Dolly! *(Pause. The bell rings again.)* Dollee! *(Pause. The bell rings twice as long as before. Lalitha goes up the stairs hesitantly.)*

LALITHA: *(calling.)* Mrs Trivedi! *(Dolly enters from her bedroom, wiping her face with a towel.)*

DOLLY: *(calling.)* Yes, I'm coming! *(To Lalitha.)* Without fail, she calls me when I'm in the bathroom. Why don't you go and speak to her? In there. Tell her I'm coming in a minute. *(Dolly exits to the bedroom. Lalitha hesitantly exits to Baa's room.)*

BAA: *(off.)* Oh, Dolly? You have come? *(Empty stage for a moment. The front door opens and Alka Trivedi enters. She is a few years younger than her sister. She is dressed to go out.)*

ALKA: Dolly? *(Exits to the kitchen, re-enters and is about to go up the stairs. Stops, moves to the phone instead and dials.)* Hello. Sridhar? Mrs Alka Trivedi. Could I speak to my husband please? ... Still busy? They are supposed to come here. Ask him when are they planning to leave... Yes, put him on... *(Looks around for Dolly.)* Nitin? I'm ready. When are you coming? *(Surprised.)* Where are we going? You were the one who said we have to go. It's for business and all that and now you say... No. Nobody told me anything... Dolly? No. She didn't say a thing to me and we were together all afternoon... Oh. When did it get cancelled? ... *(Pleading.)* Nitin, let us go somewhere. Just the two of us... just for a drive. Anywhere. There are so many things I want to discuss but we are never... I'm all dressed and ready and all you have to do is pick me up. Forget Dolly. Forget your brother! ... *(Sighs.)* All right. I will keep Baa company... Yes, I know, she's lonely! *(Hangs up. She moves slowly to the stereo and plays Naina Devi's thumri. She listens to the soulful rendition of the love song. She then moves to the kitchen area. She hesitates, then goes in. A kitchen light is switched on. The light spills onto the stage. Lalitha comes out of Baa's room. She comes down and moves slowly towards the kitchen. She exits to the kitchen. After a while Alka enters, looking flustered, followed by a bewildered Lalitha muttering an apology. Alka turns off the music.)*

LALITHA: I'm sorry. I – I didn't mean to startle you!

ALKA: Oh no, no. It's okay!

LALITHA: I didn't know you were–

ALKA: *(speaking over Lalitha.)* It's okay! I guess I was slightly – well, I usually like to open our back door and take in some cool air – It's just that I was dreaming a bit when you came and well – I admit you did startle me! *(Laughs in an embarrassed manner.)*

LALITHA: I thought you were your sister. I mean I came looking for your sister, but it was – you! *(Also laughs in an embarrassed manner.)*

ALKA: Well, I guess you'd better shut it.

LALITHA: Shut what?

ALKA: The back door. We have tons of mosquitoes over here.

LALITHA: Oh, the back door. Yes, we get mosquitoes–

ALKA: And you can switch off the light as well.

LALITHA: Oh, sure! *(Exits to the kitchen. Alka quickly rushes to the bar and opens a bottle of rum.)*

(Off.) Where's the switch?

ALKA: *(shouting.)* To the left of the back door! Shut the door and you will find it! *(Alka takes a large gulp of the rum a replaces the bottle just as the kitchen light goes off. Lalitha enters.)* Haven't we met somewhere?

LALITHA: *(quickly.)* I'm Sridhar's wife.

ALKA: Oh yes. Lalitha. Right?

LALITHA: *(laughing.)* Right!

ALKA: Where's Dolly?

LALITHA: She's probably still getting dressed.

ALKA: Dressed?

LALITHA: To go out, I think.

ALKA: What do you mean?

LALITHA: Well, she thinks she is going out. With you all, I think. But my husband... Oh, it's all a big muddle!

ALKA: *(to herself.)* Oh. *(To Lalitha.)* My husband said Dolly knew.

LALITHA: No, she doesn't. I am sure of that.

ALKA: That's strange. Well, sit down, Lalitha.

LALITHA: *(sits down.)* I guess I will have to wait for an hour at least because my–

ALKA: Would you like a drink? *(Crosses to the bar.)* There's Pepsi and Limca, I think.

LALITHA: Oh, no, thanks. They make me burp.

ALKA: Still. Have something. Have a Pepsi. We'll share one. *(Begins to open a bottle of Pepsi.)* There are no snacks here. There must be something in the kitchen. *(The bottle opens with a pop and the drink fizzes out.)*

LALITHA: See what I mean. All that gas going into your stomach–

ALKA: So what do you do with yourself, Lalitha? *(While Lalitha is talking, Alka fills up two glasses with Pepsi and surreptitiously pours a generous portion of rum in her glass.)*

LALITHA: Oh, I keep myself occupied. I do a bit of writing. Freelance. I write an occasional woman's column for the Times. Sometimes I review cultural events. I am into meditation. And, oh yes, I grow bonsai plants – I've been growing them for years. I do a bit of creative writing as well. You know, poetry and stuff like that. Nothing great but...

ALKA: It gives you something to do.

LALITHA: *(not very pleased with the remark.)* Ya. I suppose so.

ALKA: *(puts the tray with drinks on the coffee table.)* No children?

LALITHA: Not yet. We are saving for a flat of our own.

ALKA: How nice to plan your life like that. *(Alka picks up Lalitha's glass to offer it to her, but simultaneously Lalitha picks up the other on the tray.)*

LALITHA: *(confused.)* Oh. Thanks. *(Assumes it's okay to accept the glass she's picked up. Alka freezes.)* Once we have enough for a down payment, we can easily get a loan from the housing finance corporation. *(Sips her drink. Alka crosses to the bar. Lalitha is puzzled by the taste. She sips again to confirm.)* You've put rum in mine.

ALKA: *(turns to Lalitha.)* That was my drink.

LALITHA: Oh, I'm sorry, I didn't realize that you were... *(Takes another sip of it.)* Can I have it?

ALKA: *(laughs with relief.)* Yes, of course. Er – it's not too strong?

LALITHA: A little bit. But it's all right.

ALKA: Oh. In that case... let me just add some in mine. *(Picks up the bottle of rum and brings it to where her glass is.)* I have an occasional one. It's good for digestion. *(Pours a stiff one.)*

LALITHA: I have not-so-occasional ones at parties. It's nice to get high once in a while.

ALKA: *(guardedly.)* Your husband doesn't mind?

LALITHA: No, I don't think so. *(Drinks.)* As long as he's around when it happens, he doesn't mind. You must do a bit of social drinking too.

ALKA: *(sits down.)* I don't. I don't drink at all.

LALITHA: *(puzzled.)* Oh. *(Alka and Lalitha drink.)*

ALKA: You said you make bonsai?

LALITHA: Yes. I've got a whole collection.

ALKA: How do you make them?

LALITHA: You stunt their growth. You keep trimming the roots and bind their branches with wire and... stunt them. *(The bell rings sharply.)*

ALKA: *(starts.)* Oh! That bell!

LALITHA: I forgot. Your mother-in-law was asking for Dolly. *(The bell rings again.)* Such a loud bell.

BAA: *(off.)* Dolly!

ALKA: *(worked up.)* I can hear it at my house.

LALITHA: She keeps talking to herself.

BAA: *(off.)* Dolly!

LALITHA: Maybe somebody should go up...

ALKA: She probably needs the bedpan or something – *(The bell rings.)* When she is in my house, I tell her to ring once and wait!

BAA: *(off.)* Dollee!

ALKA: I hope Dolly had the sense to feed her. She complains to her sons we don't feed her! *(Crosses to the stairway.)* And the cook isn't here for another ten days.

LALITHA: What about the replacement?

ALKA: *(freezes.)* What did you say?

LALITHA: The temporary cook or something. Will he look after her if you all are not here? *(Pause.)*

ALKA: Oh, so she told you about Kanhaiya.

LALITHA: Who? *(The bell rings. Dolly enters on the landing in a formal sari.)*

DOLLY: *(to Alka.)* I'm almost ready. Have they called or anything? Maybe they're on their way here. *(Exits to Baa's room. Alka suddenly laughs.)*

LALITHA: Shouldn't we tell her?

ALKA: Don't you dare! We'll have some fun.

LALITHA: *(uncomfortably.)* I don't know.

ALKA: Pretend you know nothing.

LALITHA: That shouldn't be too difficult.

ALKA: *(sits down and picks up her drink.)* Drink it quickly and I'll make another one for you.

LALITHA: Oh, no, thank you. One is enough for me.

ALKA: *(quickly.)* For me too. *(Alka and Lalitha drink.)* You must tell me how you make them.

LALITHA: What?

ALKA: The bonsai.

LALITHA: Oh, the bonsai. *(Dolly enters from Baa's room and exits to her own. Lalitha clears her throat.)* I suppose it comes with a bit of practice. In the beginning, you will have a lot of dead shoots on your hands. But then you learn and it – comes. Anyone can do it. You first find a sapling of your choice. It could be of any tree. *(Dolly enters with her vanity bag. She comes down the stairs while Lalitha is speaking.)* I myself prefer a fruit bearing tree because when they are fully grown *(giggles.)* I guess you can't call them fully grown, but when they've reached their *(demonstrates with her hands.)* dwarfed maturity, they really look bizarre with pea-sized mangoes or oranges! *(Dolly sits on the sofa and removes her cosmetics from the bag. She has her back to the other two.)* Anyway, then you plant the sapling in a shallow tray – you've got to make sure the roots don't have enough space to spread. You still have to keep trimming them as they grow.

ALKA: Sounds very tedious.

LALITHA: Here comes the best part. *(Dolly begins her make-up.)* You can shape their branches into whatever shape you want – by pinching or wiring the shoots.

DOLLY: Have they called?

ALKA: No, they haven't called. I would have told you if they'd called.

DOLLY: *(to Lalitha.)* Is your husband coming to pick you up?

LALITHA: Well – yes.

DOLLY: Good. Did he say anything else? Whether they are coming? *(Lalitha looks uncomfortably at Alka. Alka shakes her head. Dolly turns around.)* Did he?

LALITHA: Well, no.

DOLLY: Good. I have to do my make-up here. Jiten has fixed tubelights, of all things, in the bedroom. For all you know, the Kapoors might have tubelights. So my make-up is going to look ugly anyway. *(Lalitha looks at Alka. Dolly looks at Alka.)* Alka, your foundation looks heavy even under these lights. You are going to look ghastly under tubelights.

ALKA: How are you so sure they're going to have tubelights?

DOLLY: How are the Kapoors?

ALKA: They must be fine. How would I know?

DOLLY: I wasn't enquiring after their health. I mean what kind of people are they? You were bragging that Nitin talks to you about–

ALKA: I wasn't bragging. Why should I brag to you?

DOLLY: You're always implying–

ALKA: You said bragging first and now–

DOLLY: I don't wish to go through all that now.

ALKA: Then why did you bring it up?

DOLLY: I didn't. It was only – *(Angrily.)* All right, I will say it! You're always implying that you have a better deal than me! *(Mimics.)* Oh, didn't Jiten tell you that? Nitin told me a week ago! Or, Nitin told me all four of us were going but Jiten changed his mind!

ALKA: But that's true! There's no need to imply anything, it's a fact! At parties, you just sit in a corner sipping your lime juice and speak when spoken to. You refuse to mix, you refuse to be interesting. You are just not – an interested party. That's why they don't take us out more often.

DOLLY: Two years. It's not even two years since it happened and you still want me to believe you have a better deal?

ALKA: Don't bring that up! That has nothing to do with this! We are talking about socializing, so stick to that. *(Pause.)*

DOLLY: *(senses she has gone too far.)* You are right. I guess I must learn to be a bit more... sociable. I admit I'm not half as talkative as you are. *(To Lalitha.)* I – I guess one has to acquire these skills. Don't you think so?

LALITHA: The trick is to talk about things you know a lot about. That's what I do. Like I always talk about my bonsai, given half a chance. *(Laughs.)* It's my speciality, you could say!

DOLLY: *(putting the finishing touches to her make-up.)* I'm sorry it has been a wasted evening for you, Lalitha. Personally, I would prefer chatting with you than bragging to strangers about how many prizes Daksha has won in school.

LALITHA: *(looks at Alka, then speaks to Dolly.)* Mrs Trivedi, I think you must know–

ALKA: Call me Alka. Mrs Trivedi sounds too formal.

DOLLY: Yes. Besides it would be less confusing. We won't know who you are addressing if you call us both 'Mrs Trivedi'. *(Examines her make-up in a hand. mirror.)* There. Just a hint. Nothing too heavy. *(Looks at Alka.)* Alka, you can definitely do with a little less of everything. Use my cleansing milk and take it all off. I will do your make-up for you.

ALKA: There's no need. I don't have to.

LALITHA: Mrs Trivedi – Dolly...

DOLLY: What do you mean you don't have to? You don't want to.

ALKA: We are not going.

DOLLY: Oh, don't be so stubborn!

ALKA: We are not going because it has been called off! Both you and me – we are going nowhere! Is that clear?

DOLLY: Who called it off?

ALKA: Does it matter? *(Smugly.)* We are not going. That's it.

DOLLY: You knew! You knew and you didn't tell me!

ALKA: You knew. You knew and you forgot. Nitin told me you knew!

DOLLY: How could I forget such a thing? You know I was looking forward to it. We haven't been out since God knows when.

ALKA: *(laughs.)* And you just said you would prefer talking to Lalitha than brag about Daksha's school prizes!

DOLLY: *(angrily.)* Leave her out of this!

ALKA: Who? Lalitha?

DOLLY: You know perfectly well who I mean! *(To Lalitha.)* What kind of a joke is this? You two watch calmly while I get dressed and now you tell me.

LALITHA: I wasn't very sure myself!

ALKA: Jiten had told you but you didn't want to believe it!

DOLLY: If Jiten had told me, I would have been happy to talk about the ball with Lalitha. In my housecoat.

ALKA: So that's what you can do now.

DOLLY: *(a little tearfully.)* He never told me! He never told me anything! (*Crosses to the phone and dials. The bell rings sharply.)*

BAA: *(off.)* Dolly!

ALKA: There's one person who is dead sure she isn't going out.

DOLLY: Go see what she wants.

ALKA: She is calling for you. *(The bell rings again, a little longer. Alka covers her ears.)* I'm coming! *(Moves towards the staircase.)* God should fix her arms as well so she can't ring that wretched bell! Two things she fights us all with. That bell and her loud mouth! *(Exits to Baa's room.)*

BAA: *(off.)* Oh, Dolly? You have come?

DOLLY: *(on the phone.)* Hello, Sridhar? *(Looks at Lalitha.)* Yes, she is right here... No, we haven't finished with the ball. We haven't started, in fact. Could I speak to my husband? ... He's what? ... Well, wake him up! ... *(To Lalitha.)* He's sleeping. Maybe he isn't feeling well.

LALITHA: Oh, dear.

DOLLY: *(on the phone.)* Hahn Jiten? Why aren't we going? ... No, I swear you didn't tell me! ... Well I might have been around when you spoke to them on the phone... Okay, okay, I was around. But I didn't gather they were calling it off... Sorry, right – you were calling it off... No, I don't recall. *(Sighs.)* What difference does it make whether I do or not? The fact is you didn't tell me directly... Look. Never mind the Kapoors. Let's just go out somewhere. To that new restaurant. We could all go. We will invite Lalitha and Sridhar as well. *(To Lalitha.)* Wouldn't you like to go?

LALITHA: Well, er... my husband may...

DOLLY: *(on the phone.)* Yes. Lalitha would love to come with us. I'll tell you what. We can all discuss the ball... *(Sighs.)* Don't worry. Baa has eaten... She isn't asleep yet. You know how she is. She will blabber all night if she can't get any sleep... No. No. She has been taking too much Calmpose. It's not good for her. Only if she has pain... *(Her tone changes.)* What? ... Oh... When did he come? ... Are you... doing any business with him? ... Is he coming to see us? ... Oh. Why not? ... *(Emotionally.)* It's too far! All of a sudden we've become 'too far' for him! *(Resigned.)* Okay. Come whenever you feel like. We are all here. Where would we go? *(Hangs up, a little shaken.)*

LALITHA: *(clears her throat.)* Your mother-in-law seemed a little restless. *(Dolly moves to the window slowly, lost in thought.)* I hope she is well. *(Pause.)* She looked fine. *(Pause.)* A bit restless but otherwise fine. *(Pause.)* She kept asking for someone. I forget the name. *(Dolly is looking out of the window.)* She kept asking whether he had come. The name – what was it?

DOLLY: Praful.

LALITHA: Praful! *(Pause.)*

DOLLY: *(still looking out.)* Oh no!

LALITHA: What is it?

DOLLY: That wretched woman is back. Where's that watchman? She sneaks in all the time.

LALITHA: Who?

DOLLY: I think he deliberately lets her in! *(Lalitha goes over to the window.)* If I throw her out, she will go over to Alka's house.

LALITHA: *(looks out.)* Where? I can't see anyone.

DOLLY: That bundle of tarpaulin over there. She is just a shrivelled-up old beggar woman.

LALITHA: You can hardly see her under that piece of tarpaulin.

DOLLY: She keeps shuttling between my house and Alka's. Very clever. She comes in late and leaves early.

LALITHA: Oh. What shall we do?

DOLLY: Where is that watchman? Probably fast asleep in his shelter. *(Crosses to the sofa.)* He will only wake up when he hears saab honking for him to open the gate.

LALITHA: What shall we do about the old lady?

DOLLY: *(sighs.)* We might as well discuss the ball.

LALITHA: *(crosses to the sofa.)* Yes, of course! Since we have the time, we might as well put it to good use. *(Opens her bag and removes a pen and paper.)* We have to call each of our special guests and discuss their costumes with them. We could make suggestions. We don't have to make a costume for Shirley, the ReVaTee model. She will wear a black cloak and mask which she'll remove at midnight to reveal the ReVaTee nightwear. *(Laughs.)* Do you know how they got the name ReVaTee? The chairman's wife's name is Revathi. When they were in Europe on a holiday, the French couldn't pronounce her name correctly. They used to call her Re-va-tee. Her husband decided then and there that if the company diversified into women's wear and cosmetics, he would call it the ReVaTee range. Poor Mrs Revathi Sharma.

DOLLY: You seem to take a lot of interest in your husband's work.

LALITHA: That's all he talks about at home. Even my bonsais know about ReVaTee. But I don't really mind, it gives me – *(slowing down with the realisation of what she is saying.)* – something – to – do.

DOLLY: You seem to be doing a lot of things.

LALITHA: Oh, I completely forgot! *(Opens her shopping bag.)* What with all the confusion about going out and not going out. I brought something for you. *(Takes out a bonsai of an orange tree complete with fruits.)*

DOLLY: A bonsai!

LALITHA: *(places it delicately on the coffee table.)* A small present for you from Sridhar and me.

DOLLY: *(moving to the table.)* And you made it yourself.

LALITHA: *(beams.)* Yes!

DOLLY: It looks quite – mature.

LALITHA: A couple of years.

DOLLY: Lalitha, this is sweet of you, but I'm sure this is something you value very much.

LALITHA: That is why we would like you to have it.

DOLLY: *(holds it in her palms.)* It is a complete tree! It's even borne fruit!

LALITHA: Isn't it beautiful?

DOLLY: Yes. Thank you, Lalitha. It is quite an unusual present.

LALITHA: I know. Sridhar thinks I'm crazy spending so much time over them when I could be going out and having fun. Once we won a raffle at one of those made-for-each-other contests. The prize was two free tickets to Goa or cash. Sridhar wanted Goa and I wanted cash. I just couldn't imagine leaving my bonsais with the neighbour, worrying whether she had remembered to water them. So I talked him out of it. I can be quite stubborn. Sridhar says it's typical of women to do exactly the opposite of what their husbands want, just to prove they are independent. What do you think?

DOLLY: Shall we get on with the ball?

LALITHA: Yes! Sorry if I ran on. Must be the rum.

DOLLY: Oh. You were drinking rum?

LALITHA: I have an occasional one. It sort of loosens my tongue.

DOLLY: *(taking the empty glasses to the bar.)* It seems to have worked, I notice. Do you want another one?

LALITHA: I hadn't asked for a drink. She sort of – *(Makes the motion of glasses being exchanged.)* – well, never mind. Let's get on with the ball.

ALKA: *(enters from Baa's room.)* I thought you lost sense of time when you go mad. But our mataji up there is too, too sharp. She knows she moves to my house tomorrow. You owe me a back massage. I've just given her one. When she's with me and asks for one, you better be there. My arms are aching!

DOLLY: *(going through the list.)* She doesn't feel it. So just pretend to give her one.

ALKA: She senses it!

DOLLY: Don't go on. *(To Lalitha.)* Some of these people I don't even know. *(Alka crosses to the bar.)* You do the calling.

LALITHA: I think it would be more appropriate if you called them.

ALKA: Another Pepsi, Lalitha?

LALITHA: Oh no, thank you. *(To Dolly.)* I've put my suggestions on the side.

ALKA: What about you, Dolly?

DOLLY: You know I don't drink. *(Refers to the list.)* Yes, I can imagine the Kotharis in Roman togas.

ALKA: I didn't ask you whether you wanted to drink. I asked whether you wanted a Pepsi!

DOLLY: We know perfectly well what you meant, so don't pretend. *(Refers to the list.)* Who are the Sens?

ALKA: Pretend? Why should I pretend? If I wanted to offer you a drink, I would ask you, 'Dolly, do you want a rum?' or 'Dolly, the usual whisky and water for you?' or 'How would you like your gin tonight, Dolly?' But I know you don't drink, so why should I ask you all that? Pretend! Hmpf.

DOLLY: *(nastily.)* How do you want yours? Soda, neat or on the sly? Take it whichever way you want and leave us alone.

ALKA: When have I denied it? Have you ever heard anyone asking me, 'Alka, do you drink?' And me replying, 'No, I don't?' Have you? Have you? Huh?

DOLLY: No, you don't deny you drink! It's how much you drink that you keep a closely guarded secret!

ALKA: Ha! A closely guarded secret! *(Opens the bottle of rum.)* And I guard it very closely. *(Pours out a large one.)* And I – *(closing the bottle.)* – close it very guardedly. And I – secret it very closely. *(Drinks. Dolly stares at Alka.)*

LALITHA: *(nervously.)* They are Bengalis.

DOLLY: Who?

LALITHA: The Sens. They're Bengalis. They've moved in recently. Mr Alok Sen's got a transfer from Cal. Sridhar is trying to get the account for their computer division.

DOLLY: *(looking at Alka all the time.)* You are drunk already.

ALKA: Don't worry. I'll sober up before they come.

DOLLY: *(picks up the list.)* The Mehtas will be fine as Banjaras. *(Pause. Lalitha is uncomfortable. Dolly speaks sharply.)* Don't you think so?

LALITHA: *(timidly.)* Yes. That's why I mentioned it. *(Alka is restless. She moves to the sofa, sits down, gets up again and crosses to the stereo.)*

DOLLY: *(watching Alka.)* Will we have time to make all these costumes?

LALITHA: I'm sure most of them will have their own tailors. We need help only those who ask for it.

DOLLY: Yes. And make sure everyone has a costume.

ALKA: Stop it!

DOLLY: *(going through the list.)* The Shahs as astronauts, the Bedis as Laila-Majnu, the Mendens as Hansel and Gretel. Mr Kashikar as Shivaji, the Dutts as Raj Kapoor and Nargis.

ALKA: Stop that! Stop!

DOLLY: *(suddenly, to Alka.)* You know, you make me sick! Do you know why?

ALKA: No!

DOLLY: Praful was in town and he didn't come to see us!

ALKA: Praful was in town?

DOLLY: Now you know why you make me…

ALKA: I am to blame for that? Praful comes to town and doesn't visit us, and I make you sick?

DOLLY: *(rises.)* He said it's too far! He said it's too far, but we both know the real reason.

ALKA: It is! That's the real reason!

DOLLY: Oh – come on! He comes to town and can't come here? To see his own sisters?

ALKA: *(hysterically.)* All right! He doesn't want to come!

DOLLY: And you know why, don't you?

ALKA: Say it! Say it and shut up!

DOLLY: He doesn't want to because–

ALKA: Because of me? He is dying to meet you but he won't come because of me!

DOLLY: Yes! Yes, that's right! Because of what happened the last time. And I won't go into that now if you don't want to. Oh, don't you feel humiliated at least?

ALKA: Yes! It was humiliating then. But to say that he won't come to see us because of that is even more–It's not good, what you said!

DOLLY: I can't hold it back any longer. Why should I when you can't restrain yourself? He had only come for a day. He was leaving the next morning. Couldn't you control yourself for one day?

ALKA: If I could, wouldn't I have done it? You talk as if I have no feeling of remorse.

DOLLY: Of course you couldn't help yourself! You were then just discovering the pleasures of alcohol!

ALKA: Yes. Yes!

DOLLY: I'm sorry, it just slipped out.

ALKA: He tricked me. You know it and yet you take his side.

DOLLY: You want to blame your drinking on Praful? Oh no, I won't let you get away with that.

ALKA: I was angry with him. I – I just wanted to make him feel small. I didn't think Nitin would throw me out of the house.

DOLLY: You insult your husband's mother in front of him and say you don't – you had planned it all!

ALKA: No.

DOLLY: You planned it! You waited for that chance at dinner time. You deliberately got drunk–

ALKA: I wasn't–

DOLLY: I could get that strong smell of mouthwash!

ALKA: It wasn't that way.

DOLLY: And you knew Baa would make those unpleasant remarks about our family to Praful and then you–

ALKA: *(cuts in.)* I didn't plan it…

DOLLY: And then you say some nonsense. What was it you said to Baa? In that deliberate slur! 'Your sons are so different from one another. They are both petty like you, but otherwise…' And then you wink at her and ask, 'Do they have different fathers?'

ALKA: I didn't mean that–

DOLLY: I know you didn't, but to say–

ALKA: And I didn't plan it, for God's sake! I saw, I saw them staring at each other at the table. *(Pause.)* I can't forget what they did to me! Our brother is a cheat! He lied about our father to them. And he lied to me! He lied to me by not telling me– *(Dolly slaps Alka.)*

DOLLY: *(quietly.)* He did that for your own good. You would never have been – accepted – anywhere else. You should appreciate that. *(Pause.)* For three months I was in agony after your husband threw you out. Praful came twice begging and pleading with Nitin to take you back. And I had to beg and plead with Jiten to ask his brother to do so. Poor Praful. I know you must have felt humiliated as well, but I can't help feeling that you – well…

ALKA: Deserved it.

DOLLY: But Praful didn't! What had he done to deserve such treatments? He was insulted by all three of them because of you.

ALKA: *(sarcastically.)* For you, he is the descendant of a saint! A saint! *(Laughs hard.)* Like my husband. Such close friends! Friends from college. *(Dolly gives her a look of warning.)* I didn't tell you. That time when you came home to – *(Pours herself a drink.)* – Nitin and Praful were home, talking. I came home from school with the neighbour's son on his scooter instead of walking with you. I told him to drop me before our street came. He didn't understand and dropped me right at our doorstep. Praful saw. He didn't say a word to me. He just dragged me into the kitchen. He lit the stove and pushed my face in front of it! I thought he was going to burn my face! He burnt my hair. I can still smell my hair on fire. Nitin was right behind us. Watching! Just… Praful said, 'Don't you ever look at any man. Ever.' *(Dolly takes the drink from Alka and puts it on the bar. Pause.)* He won't come to see us.

DOLLY: *(gently.)* It's too far. That's why.

ALKA: That's the real reason. Isn't it?

DOLLY: Of course. *(Alka crosses to the window. Dolly sits down again with the list.)*

ALKA: *(looking out of the window.)* She's back again.

DOLLY: The old woman? Yes. Just shout for the watchman. If he wakes up, he will throw her out. Ask him to make sure she doesn't go to your house.

ALKA: It's all right. Let her be. *(The bell rings. Alka reacts strongly. Suddenly she is angry. She shouts through the window.)* Watchman!

BAA: *(off.)* Dolly!

ALKA: Watchman!

DOLLY: *(puzzled.)* Alka? *(The bell rings again. Alka crosses to the foot of the stairs.)*

ALKA: Stop ringing that bell! *(Alka crosses to the front door. The bell rings again – five times longer than before. Alka stops and then rushes out of the front door. Silence.)*

LALITHA: *(in a small voice.)* Can I have a Pepsi? *(Clears her throat.)* It's okay, I'll help myself. *(Moves to the bar. Turns around.)* Don't you want to go see what your mother-in-law needs?

DOLLY: If she rings that bell again, I will. Help yourself!

LALITHA: I'll skip the Pepsi. *(Picks up Alka's full glass, sips the drink and looks at Dolly.)* It needs to be watered quite often.

DOLLY: What? Oh, that. *(Looks at the bonsai.)*

LALITHA: A little bit at a time. I have re-potted it, so you don't have to worry about that.

DOLLY: Does it need to be – cut or bound any more?

LALITHA: Oh no. It's completely resigned to its new shape. I suppose something happens inside it and… it decides to change its size. All it needs now is a little nourishment occasionally. You have to water it regularly. Three times a day. If you are not free, you can ask Kanhaiya to do it.

DOLLY: *(reacts sharply.)* Who?

LALITHA: Kanhaiya, your cook. *(Dolly stiffens.)* Of course, he is temporary, I forgot.

DOLLY: *(sharply.)* Alka had no business to mention – to mention Kanhaiya to you.

LALITHA: *(feigns innocence.)* Oh, but you did too!

DOLLY: Did I?

LALITHA: Is anything the matter?

DOLLY: *(under her breath.)* Yes! We shouldn't be talking about Kanhaiya to you!

ALKA: *(enters.)* I kicked her till she got up and left. *(Notices Dolly's expression.)* What's the matter? Is Baa all right?

LALITHA: *(with a hint of perverse curiosity.)* Oh, it's not Baa. We were talking about Kanhaiya.

ALKA: Oh! So you want to talk about Kanhaiya.

DOLLY: No!

ALKA: Why not?

DOLLY: I feel – embarrassed. *(Alka notices the bonsai. She goes to it and is about to pluck a fruit.)*

LALITHA: Please don't pluck the fruit. It takes very long to grow. *(Pause.)*

ALKA: All right. We can talk about Daksha.

LALITHA: *(obviously interested.)* Daksha?

ALKA: Her daughter. Didn't you know?

LALITHA: Well, she had mentioned her.

ALKA: She must like you very much. She hardly ever mentions her daughter to anyone.

DOLLY: Stop it!

ALKA: She doesn't tell anyone–

DOLLY: Stop it, I said!

ALKA: She doesn't tell anyone that her daughter is training to be a dancer! She is going to be a famous dancer, isn't she?

DOLLY: I don't want to–

ALKA: You are too modest. Let me boast about her.

DOLLY: Alka, please! Don't.

ALKA: *(crosses to Dolly.)* Please. I have to. There's – too much between just the two of us! We won't get a chance like this again!

DOLLY: *(sighs.)* I don't know.

ALKA: All right. I'll give you a choice. Either we talk about Daksha – or Kanhaiya. *(Bends to her.)* Which one will it be? *(Pause.)*

DOLLY: Kanhaiya. *(Laughs suddenly.)* This is embarrassing!

ALKA: Oh, don't be! It's only Lalitha. We are all friends now. Aren't we all friends, Lalitha?

LALITHA: Yes! What's a few words between friends?

ALKA: *(goes to the bar.)* Well said! *(Looks for her drink.)* I thought I'd left my...

LALITHA: *(giggles.)* I'm sorry, I've got it!

ALKA: No harm done, I'll just – *(Pours a rum for herself.)* You see, living so far away from the city, we have learnt to be sort of – self-sufficient. Even in our little distractions. I have plenty of distractions. At parties, for instance, I go around saying so-and-so said this about so-and-so. So naturally so-and-so calls me the next day to confirm and I, of course, deny I said anything about so-and-so to so-and-so. All very exciting.

DOLLY: And you also have the bottle.

ALKA: Yes. That too. Whereas poor Dolly is too… straight. She is neither interested in the so-and-sos of this world, nor unfortunately, in the bottle. Poor Dolly, sitting all by herself, looking pretty and… wasted. With only a half-dead mother-in-law for company. And a toothless cook. But then one day, the toothless old cook's father dies and he has to go to his village. But what luck! You see, he sends this replacement who is not so toothless.

LALITHA: *(tipsy.)* Our Kanhaiya.

ALKA: Kanhaiyalal. The toothless cook's friend's grandson. Only twenty.

DOLLY: Nineteen.

ALKA: Oh that's even better. A teenager still. *(Looks at Dolly.)* Just a few years older than Daksha.

DOLLY: Don't be disgusting.

ALKA: Sorry, I couldn't resist.

LALITHA: They mature fast in the villages.

ALKA: Yes! Absolutely! Our Kanhaiya looks really – ripe.

DOLLY: You are crude!

ALKA: How would you describe him?

DOLLY: Beautiful.

ALKA: Beautiful. Our Dolly's beautiful little Kanhaiya. Can I call him that?

DOLLY: *(closes her eyes.)* Just go on.

ALKA: Five days – or nights. *(To Lalitha.)* When everything gets really quiet, and the husbands have gone to the club, and Baa has been fed – Dolly plays a love song.

DOLLY: Thumri.

ALKA: Same thing.

DOLLY: Naina Devi, the queen of thumri. What a voice! So rich and so–

ALKA: Appropriate.

DOLLY: Yes!

ALKA: So Dolly plays this appropriate thumri… No, wait. I can't hear it yet! You see, I'm watching from my bedroom window which overlooks her backyard so… so what do I see? *(Walks behind Dolly.)* The light outside the kitchen is on and I can see very clearly. I see Kanhaiya. Sitting on his haunches on the parapet outside his room. Spitting on the plants below. The light outside the kitchen goes off. I can't see him now! Only the lit end of his beedi which glows brighter when he puffs on it. He will finish it and then retire for the night. But wait. The light inside the kitchen comes on! And the kitchen door opens. I can see him again. And I can hear the thumri now. Faintly. Dolly comes to the door. In her pale blue nightie. The light behind her. I don't see the lit beedi anymore. That's because he has cupped it in his hand, embarrassed to be seen smoking. He looks away, waiting for her to ask for something or go away. She doesn't. He can't help but look at her. He can easily see the lines of her body, with the light behind her. Could it be? Or is it his imagination? He probably wonders. Perhaps he wishes he could see her face. For familiar signals.

DOLLY: Oh no, there are none!

ALKA: He decides to find out. He flicks his beedi away, jumps off the parapet and slowly walks towards her. Head bent so as not to betray his intentions. He asks her something.

DOLLY: He asks whether he can make me some tea. And I say, 'Come in.'

ALKA: She moves a little to let him in. He strides in, very confident now. Dolly shuts the door. The kitchen light goes off. I can't hear the thumri anymore.

DOLLY: The thumri plays. And it ends. Another one plays. I forget when that ends and a new one begins! All I'm aware of are two powerful black arms around me and the beautiful sound of the heartbeat of a warm gentle soul. The voice of Naina Devi comes back. It is the most beautiful song I've ever heard in my life! *(silence. Alka crosses to the kitchen.)*

ALKA: It's time.

DOLLY: Hmm?

ALKA: Your secret meeting.

DOLLY: What are you saying?

ALKA: It's always been the same time. For five nights.

DOLLY: *(sits up.)* No. Not tonight.

ALKA: Why? Why not tonight?

DOLLY: I won't. *(Pause.)* I sent him away.

ALKA: No, you did not!

DOLLY: I gave him the day off. He is not there.

ALKA: He came back.

DOLLY: No, he did not!

ALKA: I saw him. When I went to kick the old lady out, I saw him. He's back!

DOLLY: *(looks at Alka.)* No.

ALKA: He is back. So play your thumri, put on the kitchen light and open the back door! *(Pause.)* I'm sure he would love to see you dressed so grandly for a change.

DOLLY: You go.

ALKA: I can't.

DOLLY: You want to.

ALKA: No.

LALITHA: Of course she wants to. I saw! I saw you when you came in. *(To Dolly.)* She went straight to the kitchen and opened the back door! *(Dolly looks at Alka. Alka backs away.)*

DOLLY: You want to. And you want me to push you into going. *(The bell rings. Dolly goes to the stereo and plays the thumri softly.)*

BAA: *(off.)* Dolly! *(Alka slowly turns and moves towards the kitchen.)*

(off.) Dolly! *(Alka exits. The kitchen light comes on. The bell rings. The general lights start fading out slowly. Suddenly Alka staggers in.)*

ALKA: Noo! I can't! *(Sits on the sofa, crying.)* Praful, your sister is good. She's good. *(Lalitha moves to her. Dolly looks at her for a moment, and then slowly walks towards the kitchen.)*

BAA: *(off.)* Dollee! *(Dolly exits. The music continues. Slow fade out.)*

ACT 2

The Men

(The offices of Jiten and Nitin Trivedi. An advertising agency. Pin-ups of campaigns on a board. A huge photograph of a sensuous model with the ReVaTee logo. Two large desks with executive chairs. A comfortable couch next to Jiten's desk. A smaller desk belonging to Sridhar, which is overcrowded with papers and assorted items. There is also a rather odd-looking bonsai on his table. One doorway leads to the reception area, another to the toilet. The level representing Baa's room remains as in Act I. So does the well-stocked bar. The Act opens with Nitin is going through accounts. Jiten is leaning on his table, smoking, going through some photographs.)

NITIN: Damn these computers! There are multiple entries on every page.

JITEN: *(without looking up.)* Give it back to the accountant tomorrow. What do we pay that asshole for?

NITIN: It's time one of us went through them. *(Mutters.)* Always in the red. No matter how much money we earn…

JITEN: *(tosses a photograph on Nitin's desk.)* Take a look at this one.

NITIN: What for?

JITEN: The ReVaTee model.

NITIN: What did you say?

JITEN: The new ReVaTee model.

NITIN: Are you serious?

JITEN: *(walks to the ReVaTee model's photograph.)* I'm pissed off with this one.

NITIN: *(looks relieved.)* Oh, that's all. For a moment I thought you were serious.

JITEN: For the commercial we can use another one.

NITIN: This is the last big account we have. So let's try to keep it. The client will never accept a different face halfway through a campaign.

JITEN: She's modelling undies. Who the hell will notice the face?

NITIN: Sridhar will tell you why we can't do that.

JITEN: I'm asking you. Who cares a shit what Sridhar thinks?

NITIN: *(looks at him.)* I think Shirley is very good.

JITEN: Ya? You think so?

NITIN: She is right for the product. She has the right image.

JITEN: I guess we are stuck with her. Where is this bugger?

NITIN: *(going through the accounts.)* He should be here now. Tonight, wasn't it?

JITEN: What?

NITIN: He said he would take his wife over to your place. To discuss the ball.

JITEN: What's her name?

NITIN: Lalitha. Was it tonight?

JITEN: *(crosses to the couch.)* Maybe.

NITIN: The ball was a good idea. Make all the top shots happy.

JITEN: At the client's expense. And get this Shirley girlie to strip at the end.

NITIN: Jitu, let's talk finance before Sridhar gets here.

JITEN: Fix me a whisky.

NITIN: *(crosses over to the bar.)* It's bad.

JITEN: I know.

NITIN: You have to go through the figures–

JITEN: I don't have to go through the figures. I know.

NITIN: *(pours a whisky.)* We can't let this account go.

JITEN: Who said anything about letting it go? That's what Sridhar's there for. To see we don't lose it.

NITIN: Then I think we should leave it all to him instead of interfering with the campaign. We know nothing about the line.

JITEN: Hmm hmm. Can't. Sometimes he gets too much masti. There was no need for that bloody market survey with all those dames. Mustn't let him think he can do everything on his own.

NITIN: I'm more worried about the money.

JITEN: Don't. Where's my drink?

NITIN: *(moves to Jiten.)* Tomorrow I have to sit here answering those calls. *(Hands Jiten his drink.)*

JITEN: I have thought of something.

NITIN: We already owe the banks and the finance corporation.

JITEN: *(drinks.)* Don't worry, I said.

NITIN: What are you thinking of? *(No response.)* If it's a private borrowing, we are sunk for the rest of our lives.

JITEN: *(looks at his drink distastefully.)* Nothing to beat Black Label.

NITIN: *(goes to the bar.)* Thirty-six percent. Nichani will want nothing less.

JITEN: We are not taking the money from Nichani. This tastes like pee.

NITIN: Jitu, we can't afford the interest.

JITEN: We won't have to pay him any interest.

NITIN: Oh. What does he want? A partnership?

JITEN: *(lights a cigarette.)* No. He doesn't want anything in return.

NITIN: When does he want it back?

JITEN: Payable when able.

NITIN: *(drinks.)* A favour. Something we'll have to return sooner or later.

JITEN: No.

NITIN: Nobody does anything for nothing.

JITEN: He will. *(Pause.)*

NITIN: Who's the joker?

JITEN: *(blows a smoke ring.)* Praful. *(Pause.)*

NITIN: Like I said, nobody does anything for nothing.

JITEN: He is different. He's a sentimental fool.

NITIN: No fool makes big money overnight.

JITEN: When it comes to his sisters, he can't think straight.

NITIN: No.

JITEN: I know what you're thinking. Alka will never let you forget this. Right? *(Nitin nods.)* And this is Praful's way of showing that he is a better human being than us. We insult him and treat him like a piece of shit but he, when his turn comes, actually helps us out. Right? *(No response.)* Sentimental fool. *(Drinks.)* I can take his money and still treat him like crap. He is nothing. The very fact that he needs to show he is capable of helping us proves he is nothing. He is so inferior that he has to prove himself by loaning us ten lakhs!

NITIN: When did you speak to him?

JITEN: He called yesterday. You were here.

NITIN: I – I was going through the accounts.

JITEN: *(nods.)* He himself offered to loan us. I told him we needed ten. He said he can arrange it. He said he wouldn't dream of taking interest, after all, we are his brothers-in-law!

NITIN: Bastard!

JITEN: *(sarcastically.)* We need the bastard's money.

NITIN: Did he speak to Dolly?

JITEN: She was with Alka. I told him they had gone out. *(Pause.)*

NITIN: All right – I agree. On one condition.

JITEN: What?

NITIN: Alka mustn't know. Neither of them should.

JITEN: That's no problem.

NITIN: Make that clear to Praful.

JITEN: I won't tell him any such thing. Tell him that we don't want our wives to know about it? That's just the sort of thing he is waiting to hear.

NITIN: Then how? He is bound to mention something to them.

JITEN: Leave that to me. *(Goes to the phone and dials.)*

NITIN: Ask for twelve. We can circulate the extra two on interest.

JITEN: Brilliant. *(On the phone, putting on a phony British accent.)* Hullow. Could you give me room – *(Searches around on his table, continues in a normal voice.)* – shit, where's his room number? *(On the phone. Puts on an accent again.)* Mr Praful Shah from Bombay… Yes. Thank you… *(To Nitin, in a normal voice.)* Bitch. They love it when you put on an accent… *(On the phone.)* Hahn. Praful? Bol… Yes, I have discussed it with Nitin…You can come over here. We are in the office right now… At home? … *(Nitin gestures to say 'no'. Jiten motions to indicate he has understood.)* Er, Praful. We won't be home till very late. I'll tell you what. It's not fair to make you come all the way. We will come to your hotel tomorrow morning… Dolly and Alka? No, they've gone to Ooty with some friends – Oh well, why should I hide anything from you, after all we are doing business together. So I'll tell you the truth. You see Baa and your sisters are not exactly – you know, the usual problems. And Alka being so – of course, Baa is to blame as well. She shouldn't keep bringing up your background. It's not fair. But you know how old people are. So your presence will only… Please don't misunderstand. I'm sure Baa will be happy to know that we are doing business together. Dolly and Alka also. But let me handle them. Leave it to me. I'II tell you what – why don't you join us at the club tomorrow? We will do a bit of boozing and gup-shup. It's been a long time! *(Laughs heartily.)* So it's pukka. We will see you in the morning… Oh, by the way, make it twelve instead of ten. I hope that's not a problem for you… I Oh, no problem. You can give the rest next week. We will see you in the morning… Thanks… Oh, you are welcome. Bye! *(Hangs up and looks at Nitin smugly.)*

NITIN: We'll throw it back on his face, once the campaign is through and the client gives us an advance.

JITEN: Even if it isn't through, we can pack up this agency.

NITIN: Pack up? No.

JITEN: Why spend so much money in running an agency without a solid client?

NITIN: The ReVaTee account should be worth at least fifty.

JITEN: If we get it.

NITIN: Jitu, we need this office. It's the only office we have. Without it we won't have any kind of – credibility as businessmen.

JITEN: Without the account we can't.

NITIN: We will get it.

JITEN: *(moves to Sridhar's desk.)* I don't like the way this Sridhar is handling it.

NITIN: Why, what's the matter with how–?

JITEN: The chooth says it's all wrong. The client doesn't like it.

NITIN: Let him come and we'll sort things–

JITEN: *(angrily.)* If he can't get a client to like the campaign, what use is he?

NITIN: There must be some reason why–

JITEN: They can all go jump! They don't like it. Bullshit! *(Sweeps his hand over Sridhar's table. All the papers fly about.)* We don't need this shit! *(Sridhar enters, carrying a helmet and wearing a windcheater.)*

SRIDHAR: Careful! Don't knock the bonsai! *(Sridhar picks up the bonsai as if to protect it from Jiten. Jiten stares at the bonsai and then at Sridhar.)*

JITEN: *(to Sridhar.)* Clear up all this. *(Exits to the toilet.)*

SRIDHAR: Am I late? I dropped Lalitha and came straight here.

NITIN: *(looks in Jiten's direction.)* No. You're on time.

SRIDHAR: *(picking up the papers.)* Why did he do this? *(The telephone rings.)*

NITIN: *(lighting a cigarette.)* Answer it. *(Sridhar answers the phone. Throughout the conversation, he tries to pick up the remaining papers.)*

SRIDHAR: *(on the phone.)* Hello? Lalitha? Just got in. Ya. What? … Mixed up what dates? … Is she there? … Then what's your problem? … They? Who's they? *(Looks at Nitin.)* Yes, but they are here… Look, I think she has got her dates mixed up… One sec… *(To Nitin.)* Were you all planning to go out?

NITIN: It was called off. Dolly knows. Let me talk to her.

SRIDHAR: *(on the phone.)* Give the phone to Mrs Trivedi… Oh. *(To Nitin.)* She is getting dressed to go out. *(Nitin is puzzled. He crosses to the toilet.)*

SRIDHAR: *(on the phone.)* What can I do?

NITIN: *(shouting to Jiten.)* Did you inform Dolly it was called off?

JITEN: *(off.)* For God's sake, let me pee in peace!

SRIDHAR: *(on the phone.)* Doesn't look like anybody's going out.

NITIN: Jitu, did you tell her or not?

JITEN: *(off.)* Of course I did. Nobody's going anywhere!

SRIDHAR: *(on the phone.)* Nobody's going anywhere… because I say so! You might as well discuss the ball… *(Nitin walks towards Sridhar.)* All right! Do what you want. I'll pick you up in an hour… No. Can't. I've got work… Ya… Fine… Do that. Bye. *(Hangs up. Sridhar continues to pick up his papers. He notices Nitin looking at the bonsai.)* My wife keeps making them. She gives them to people she likes. And converts them to plant lovers. *(Nitin continues to stare at it.)* Is anything the matter?

NITIN: Nothing. I just remembered someone who liked… huge trees. *(Pause.)* My father. *(Baa's area is suddenly lit. She presses a switch, but the bell cannot be heard. Baa is in her late sixties. She is covered up to her waist with a blanket. There are pillows propping her up. There is a wheelchair next to her bed.)*

SRIDHAR: I don't know whether these can be called trees anymore. *(Baa mouths the word 'Dolly'. We don't hear her yet. This is quite an odd one. Baa presses the switch again and mouths 'Dolly'. She waits and presses again.)* Lalitha tells me that the trunk is supposed to look about the same shape as the actual size tree. This one is grotesque. It happens when you don't bind it or shape it correctly.

NITIN: It looks – interesting.

SRIDHAR: Do you want it?

NITIN: What will I do with it?

SRIDHAR: You could give it to your wife. I know Lalitha has taken one as a gift for your sister-in-law. So…

NITIN: No. What will she do with it? *(Sits at his desk. On the higher level, Lalitha enters Baa's room very hesitantly.)*

BAA: Oh, Dolly? You have come?

LALTHA: Dolly will be here in a minute.

BAA: Dolly, come. Rub my head–

LALITHA: I'm not Dolly.

BAA: Not Dolly? Then?

LALITHA: I – I'm Lalitha.

BAA: *(her face lights up.)* Oh, Lally! Where have you been, Lally?

LALITHA: I'm not Lally. I'm Lalitha. My husband works–

BAA: You are Lally? Padma's daughter? No?

LALITHA: No.

BAA: Oh! I'm so happy you are not Padma's Lally. Padma's Lally is dead. *(The telephone rings. Sridhar answers it.)*

SRIDHAR: *(on the phone.)* Hello? ... Yes, he is here. Just a minute. *(To Nitin.)* It's your wife.

LALITHA: Can I help you?

NITIN: *(on the phone.)* Hello? Ya.

BAA: Where's Praful?

LALITHA: Who?

BAA: Dolly, where is your brother?

LALITHA: I'm not Dolly! Dolly will be–

BAA: You are not Dolly. You are not Lally. Who are you?

NITIN: But where do you think we are going?

LALITHA: Dolly is dressing up. They are going out.

BAA: Those girls go out, go out, go out aaall the time!

LALITHA: I think their husbands wanted them to.

NITIN: *(rudely.)* Hasn't anybody told you?

BAA: Oh! Jitu and Nitin are taking them out?

NITIN: No. Dolly knows.

BAA: My Nitin is afraid of going out in the dark.

NITIN: That's very strange.

LALITHA: Did you need anything?

NITIN: I can't. We are working.

BAA: Ten years old and he is still afraid of the dark. Afraid to sleep in the dark. Afraid of his father – who is as black as night!

NITIN: I think you should keep Baa company. She is lonely. *(Hangs up. Simultaneously, the spotlight in Baa's area goes off. Jiten enters from the toilet, wiping his face with his handkerchief.)*

JITEN: *(going straight to the bar.)* Right. Let's get this ReVaTee thing straight. Another one for you, Nitin?

NITIN: *(lights a cigarette.)* Don't mind.

JITEN: *(pouring two whiskies.)* Go on. I'm listening. Sridhar!

SRIDHAR: What? Oh, sorry. *(Rises and moves in front of his table.)* I went to the director's meeting today. I showed them the AV for the fourth time. I'm sorry. The answer is still negative.

JITEN: What did Menon say?

SRIDHAR: He just sat on the fence.

JITEN: He needs his arse poked.

NITIN: Ten per cent for saying yes. How much more poking does he need?

SRIDHAR: Perhaps the problem is not the kickback.

JITEN: *(gives Nitin his drink.)* What is it, then?

SRIDHAR: *(cautiously.)* I think they genuinely didn't like it.

NITIN: You keep saying that. Why?

JITEN: They didn't like the model? We can dump her.

SRIDHAR: No, no. The model is fine.

JITEN: Then what's wrong?

SRIDHAR: They said something strange.

NITIN: Strange?

SRIDHAR: Odd

JITEN: What did they say?

SRIDHAR: They liked the presentation.

JITEN: *(testily.)* What did they say?

SRIDHAR: It was the concept, I think.

NITIN: They found the concept odd?

JITEN: Just repeat what they said! *(Pause.)*

SRIDHAR: They said we – haven't understood women. *(Silence.)*

JITEN: Who do they think we are? Dodos?

SRIDHAR: *(uncomfortably.)* One of them said the campaign lacked soul.

NITIN: And you? What do you think?

SRIDHAR: *(clears his throat.)* It's hard to explain.

NITIN: Go on.

SRIDHAR: Well, to start with... the product. Nightwear and underwear. Colour-coordinated. Exclusive designs. Exclusive market. All very fancy. Now, why would a woman go in for something expensive if she is going to wear it only at night? Primarily for sexual reasons.

NITIN: That is what our campaign is geared towards – sex.

SRIDHAR: Precisely. And that is where it has failed.

JITEN: *(with a cigarette between his lips.)* Give me a light.

NITIN: *(lights the cigarette.)* Go on.

SRIDHAR: You see, take our press ads. You've got the model lying invitingly on a bed and the signature is 'Light his Fire with ReVaTee.' In the storyline for the video commercial, you have the model looking out of the window and she sees that her husband or her lover has come home. She quickly rushes, opens a box, removes the new ReVaTee bra, panties and nightie. Cut to her dressed in them. She lets her hair loose, pirouettes and lies down on the bed, just as the door opens. Freeze. Signature 'Light his Fire with ReVaTee.'

JITEN: It's a hit. A sure success!

SRIDHAR: I told you about the market survey. About a dozen women. A cross-section of upper-middle class, upper class and the stinking rich. We had given them a questionnaire each to fill up after seeing the AV. We needn't go through all of them. *(Searches for them.)* I had it all computed on one analysis chart. Where is it?

NITIN: Just tell us what they said.

SRIDHAR: I wanted to read out the detailed analysis. All my papers are mixed up!

JITEN: Sort them out tomorrow. Get on with it.

SRIDHAR: I can tell you what the bottom line was. They all said – in different words of course – but most of them used one word to describe it – offensive. They all found it highly offensive.

JITEN: Bull.

SRIDHAR: I tried explaining to the directors today that women may not mean what they say, and in our experiences with various products, we've come across layers of complexities in consumer behaviour, and that this kind of survey had its limitations and may not work for all products. And this ad will appeal to latent subconscious desires and not overt, superficial, culturally-bound responses.

NITIN: What did they say?

SRIDHAR: Bull. That's when somebody said we haven't understood women. *(Sighs.)* I tried my best. I promised them another presentation. In a week's time. *(Pause.)* So? Do we do it? Can you arrange the money?

JITEN: The money isn't your concern.

SRIDHAR: Good. I'll inform the copy chief. They can start work on it right from tomorrow.

JITEN: No.

SRIDHAR: Are they busy with something else? I think this should get top priority.

JITEN: No.

SRIDHAR: You don't think this deserves top priority.

JITEN: We are not making another presentation.

NITIN: Jitu.

SRIDHAR: Why?

JITEN: They can either take this one or shove it.

SRIDHAR: Are you serious? You must be joking!

NITIN: *(gestures to Sridhar to stop.)* Jitu, shall we discuss this on our own?

JITEN: There's nothing to discuss. I think it's a great campaign.

SRIDHAR: They hated it!

JITEN: They just need pushing.

SRIDHAR: I pushed them enough.

JITEN: Not hard enough!

SRIDHAR: But the consumer survey clearly showed–

JITEN: Screw the survey! You know who you should have tested it out on? Men!

SRIDHAR: Men!

JITEN: Yes! Men would want to buy it for their women! That's our market. Men. Men would want their women dressed up like that. And they have the buying power. Yes! So there's no point in asking a group of screwed-up women what they think of it. They'll pretend to feel offended and say, 'Oh, we are always being treated like sex objects.'

SRIDHAR: Somehow I can't believe – I think we should seriously look at the questionnaires the women filled up.

JITEN: I think you should seriously have another talk with the clients.

SRIDHAR: *(searching his papers.)* Let's just look at them–

NITIN: Leave it for now, Sridhar.

JITEN: And this time push harder!

NITIN: Leave it!

SRIDHAR: I think we might as well thrash it out now since–

NITIN: *(cuts in.)* Never mind!

SRIDHAR: Wait. Let me get another print-out from the computer. *(Exits.)*

NITIN: *(taking empty glasses to the bar.)* Jitu. We need the account badly. And we need it now. If we can get it *(looks at Jiten.)* we don't need Praful's money. *(Spotlight on Baa. Dolly enters Baa's room.)*

BAA: Oh, Dolly? You have come back? So soon?

DOLLY: I hadn't gone out.

BAA: Oh? But Lally told me you were going out.

DOLLY: No, I haven't.

BAA: That Lally has always been a liar. Lying Lally!

DOLLY: Your sons are taking us out.

BAA: Is Praful coming?

DOLLY: *(sharply.)* Why? What difference does it make to you? *(Laughs suddenly.)* I know. I know we are not going out. I heard. But I'll pretend I don't know. How would I know it's been cancelled? He didn't tell me. I'm going to get dressed and wait. And pretend. *(Exits.)*

BAA: She is not going out? Good girl! *(Nitin gives Jiten his drink.)* They are always spending money, going out. Buying this and buying that. Jitu wants to go to the cinema and Nitin wants ice cream.

NITIN: We must please the client.

JITEN: Do they know what they want?

BAA: Jitu wants to see cinema and eat ice cream. I will speak to his father. Giving him so much money.

JITEN: We don't need to take this kind of crap from anyone! With the ten-twelve we are getting from Praful, we could scrap it all, pay off our debts and rotate the rest.

NITIN: And then?

BAA: Wait! What are you doing?

JITEN: Baa isn't going to live longer than a year.

BAA: No, no! Don't hit them! They're only boys! They didn't steal! Nitin, tell him you didn't steal it!

NITIN: I don't want to sell the old house. Ever.

JITEN: One and a half crores. At today's market.

BAA: I gave them the money! Yes, I took it from your purse and gave it to them!

NITIN: That's where we grew up.

BAA: Why should I not? It is my money!

NITIN: Too many memories.

JITEN: Sentimental fool.

BAA: Mine! Every paisa is mine! Mine from my father!

NITIN: It – it belongs to Daksha. Maybe we should do it up and all live there.

BAA: This is my house! My house!

NITIN: We could sell the twin houses.

JITEN: No! I built them. We built them. They are ours!

BAA: Don't shout! Who are you to shout at me?

JITEN: I'll never live in the old house.

NITIN: Why not?

JITEN: Too many memories.

BAA: You hit me? I only speak the truth and you hit me? Go on. Hit me again. The children should see what a demon you are. Aah! Jitu! Nitin! Are you watching? See your father! *(Jerks her face as if she's been slapped.)* No! No! Not on the face! What will the neighbours say? Not on the face. I beg you! Hit me but not on... aaaah! *(Covers her face weakly as her scream turns silent and the light on her fades out.)*

SRIDHAR: *(enters with the print-outs.)* Here. I've got their opinions.

JITEN: Forget it.

SRIDHAR: I'll just read out the imp–

JITEN: No.

SRIDHAR: There are only twelve of them. It won't take very long.

JITEN: I didn't say 'No, I don't have the time.' I said 'No, I don't want to read them!'

SRIDHAR: But why?

JITEN: That's none of your damn–

NITIN: Jitu, I think–

SRIDHAR: We've got to respect the consumer's viewpoint.

NITIN: Sridhar, we'll talk this over. So just–

JITEN: There won't be any talking over!

SRIDHAR: But we've got to understand what the consumer wants–

JITEN: Screw the consumer.

SRIDHAR: They'll screw us! If we don't come out with a campaign idea that works, we'll be dead!

JITEN: You think we can't survive without them? Huh?

NITIN: Damn!

SRIDHAR: I'll read them out. *(Reads quickly.)* To the question on initial reaction – positive or negative – they all ticked negative.

JITEN: Don't read them.

SRIDHAR: If negative, why? This one writes – the ad fails to enter a woman's world.

JITEN: *(cuts in.)* Don't. *(Jiten advances towards Sridhar saying 'don't' under his breath as Sridhar continues to speak.)*

SRIDHAR: There was nothing personal or realistic about it. *(Reads another.)* It was tasteless and degrading. Despite its westernised treatment, it upholds the silliest of all Indian notions that a woman exists to please man etc., etc. *(Reads another.)* No woman waits for her husband to arrive to change into a frilly overpriced nightie and jump into bed. If that's what lights his fire, I'd sooner buy an extinguisher.

JITEN: *(slams his hand on the papers on the desk.)* I said, don't read them!

SRIDHAR: These are valid comments!

JITEN: I don't want to read these comments. So shut up! *(Starts tearing them.)* Hypocrites! All of them! *(Places the torn bits on the table.)* Opinions. Hah!

SRIDHAR: This is professional suicide.

JITEN: Listen, you asshole. Tomorrow I want you to go back and tell them we are sticking to our original campaign. They can take it or shove it up! *(Pause.)*

SRIDHAR: You have gone mad

JITEN: You're fired.

SRIDHAR: What?

JITEN: Sacked. Look for another job tomorrow.

SRIDHAR: Hey, no! Wait! We are saving to buy a flat!

JITEN: Do you want your job?

SRIDHAR: Yes.

JITEN: So since you know which side your buns are buttered, you will go to them tomorrow and sell it to them.

SRIDHAR: Yes – sir.

JITEN: Good. That's settled. Have a drink.

SRIDHAR: Er – thank you.

JITEN: Help yourself. *(Sridhar looks at Nitin.)*

NITIN: Go on. *(Sridhar moves to the bar. Jiten sprawls on the couch.)*

SRIDHAR: *(to Nitin.)* Can I fix you one? *(Nitin raises his hand to say no. To Jiten.)* What about you – sir? *(Jiten doesn't respond. He's asleep.)*

NITIN: He will soon be snoring. Drops off to sleep in a second.

SRIDHAR: He's never like this during the day. *(Pours himself a whisky and water.)*

NITIN: Drops off in the car when I'm driving.

SRIDHAR: Must be dangerous for him to drive on his own.

NITIN: When he's driving, it's different. He doesn't sleep, he... he gets violent.

SRIDHAR: And reckless. Yes, I know.

NITIN: You do?

SRIDHAR: I noticed.

NITIN: What?

SRIDHAR: Your car. It was bashed up last month, I think. I know you are a safe driver so I assumed...

NITIN: Yes. *(Pause.)* There was this auto rickshaw driver. A powerful man. Last month we were returning from the club. Early morning. Jitu was driving. Fast. We were in the middle of town and he was driving recklessly. Our car toppled an autorickshaw parked near the road and we hit a lamp post. I saw the driver come running out of a tea shop, screaming at us. Ordering us to get out of the car. He was really – *(drags out the word, perhaps sensually.)* violent-looking. He tried to force the door open while Jitu tried to start the car. The driver grabbed him through the window. He put his forearm around his neck. He – he was a powerful man. I can still remember that strong black arm. *(Pause. Observes Sridhar, who is perhaps puzzled by this description.)* Jitu managed to start the car. He reversed and started to speed. The driver still hung on! Jitu braked suddenly, hoping to dislodge the man. I was fascinated. That arm didn't lose its grip. Jitu put the car in first gear and – sped. The driver wouldn't let go. *(A faint stutter.)* He was being d-dragged by the s-speed of the car but – he wouldn't let go. *(Pause. In a normal voice.)* Suddenly a truck appeared in front of us. There was barely enough room for truck and car to pass. I screamed out to the man to let go, otherwise he would be hit by the truck! But he didn't! Until the truck was almost on top of him. He let go just in time. It – it was a nightmare. *(Pause.)* Jitu knew what would have happened but he didn't stop the car. We drove away. *(Suddenly smiles at Sridhar.)* So it is better I drive and he sleeps. On my shoulder. Like a baby.

SRIDHAR: Interesting.

NITIN: What?

SRIDHAR: Oh, the... encounter. Was it really fascinating?

NITIN: Fascinating?

SRIDHAR: That's what you said.

NITIN: Did I? No. Why would I think it fascinating? *(Pause.)*

SRIDHAR: Last night I passed by this way. We were going to the pub with a few friends.

NITIN: Oh, and?

SRIDHAR: There was an autorickshaw parked outside.

NITIN: So?

SRIDHAR: The driver was inside the office compound.

NITIN: *(tense.)* Well. He didn't come up.

SRIDHAR: The office lights were on.

NITIN: Yes. I was here. I – I was going through the accounts. What else did you see?

SRIDHAR: He must have recognized the car. Hmm? I was just passing through. I didn't think it was important then.

NITIN: Well. It is unimportant. He didn't come up. *(Crosses to Sridhar's desk.)*

SRIDHAR: Ya, I guess I better speak to the clients tomorrow. I'll highlight the ball. They like the idea of the ball.

NITIN: *(fondles the bonsai.)* What?

SRIDHAR: The masked ball.

NITIN: Oh, yes.

SRIDHAR: The press have promised good coverage. *(Pause.)*

NITIN: You said you wanted me to take this for my wife.

SRIDHAR: Yes.

NITIN: Why?

SRIDHAR: I don't know. I just thought it would make a nice present. I brought it here because I thought it had an interesting shape.

NITIN: You called it grotesque. *(Baa's area is lit. Alka enters Baa's room.)*

BAA: Oh Dolly? You have come? *(The telephone rings. Sridhar goes to answer it.)*

ALKA: Why do you keep ringing that bell?

BAA: If I don't ring the bell, I will go to sleep.

SRIDHAR: *(on the phone.)* Hello.

ALKA: Can't you sing bhajans instead? Quietly.

SRIDHAR: Is Lalitha with you?

BAA: I sang bhajans.

SRIDHAR: Have you finished with your discussions?

BAA: So lovely was my voice!

ALKA: *(sharply.)* What do you want?

BAA: Rub my back.

SRIDHAR: *(looks at Jiten.)* Er, he is a little busy. He's sleeping… Yes… Well, I'll try. *(Crosses to the couch.)*

BAA: Rub my back and I will tell you something.

ALKA: I don't want to hear your nonsense.

BAA: If you don't, I will vomit and you will have to clean it.

JITEN: *(wakes up.)* Hmm. What?

SRIDHAR: Your wife is on the phone.

JITEN: Tell her I'm busy

SRIDHAR: I told her that already. *(Alka starts rubbing Baa's back.)*

BAA: Rub harder. *(Jiten picks up the phone.)*

ALKA: Why is it that you pick on me the most?

BAA: Not so hard.

JITEN: *(barking into the phone.)* Ya!

BAA: Tomorrow I will be in your house.

JITEN: I told you!

ALKA: You know and you are waiting to give me hell!

BAA: I don't forget bad deeds. It is in your blood to do bad!

JITEN: Don't lie! You were there when I called them!

ALKA: You can win so easily with me because you have two sons to protect you.

JITEN: I called it off! Not them!

BAA: Yes! I have been blessed with two sons. I thank God.

JITEN: Then you do remember, you lying…

ALKA: And I? I have been cursed because I don't have children. That's what you want to say!

BAA: Rub harder.

JITEN: Directly, indirectly – you knew! Then what's your problem?

ALKA: And Dolly? Dolly has been blessed because she has Daksha? *(Laughs in an ugly way.)*

BAA: Karma. It is all karma.

ALKA: Karma, my foot!

BAA: Don't say such things!

ALKA: You know why I can't have children. You won't let me. That's why!

BAA: What are you saying?

ALKA: You won't let us!

BAA: You are mad, mad, mad!

ALKA: You won't let us! You want him to hate me!

BAA: Go away! Away!

ALKA: He needs your permission to have children and by God, you won't give it to him!

JITEN: You are staying at home tonight!

BAA: Would any mother wish that for her child? God!

JITEN: How is Baa?

ALKA: Should I rub a little harder?

BAA: Jitu is just like his father. Just like him.

ALKA: And you wanted to make sure Nitin would be different.

BAA: *(pleadingly.)* Not so hard.

JITEN: Give her a Calmpose. From now on, give her a Calmpose every day. It will help her sleep better.

ALKA: *(bitterly.)* You know. You know deep down and yet you blame me.

BAA: Call your brother! Ask him to come here and take you away! *(In a slightly demented voice.)* Nitin! Don't marry her! Your friend Praful is fooling you! The older one is good for Jitu, but beware of the younger one! She is like her mother! *(The lights go out on Baa and Alka.)*

JITEN: *(on the phone, perversely.)* Oh, by the way, Praful called... Oh, no particular reason. All right, he owed us some money and it's time he returned it... No. He said he won't come home... He said it's too far... too far! What do you want me to do? Live near the railway station so your brother can save on auto fare? *(Sarcastically.)* I forget. He travels by air now... Right. Yes, stay at home. Do. that. *(Hangs up.)*

SRIDHAR: Have they finished?

JITEN: *(going to the bar.)* Huh?

SRIDHAR: Have they finished discussing the ball?

JITEN: *(pours a drink.)* Screw the ball!

SRIDHAR: *(clears his throat.)* Right. Let's just sum things up. Tomorrow I go back to the clients and tell them we should have another survey of male consumers, because they have the purchasing power. I'll push the present campaign and – hope for the best.

NITIN: You don't seem to be very convinced.

JITEN: Who cares whether he is convinced or not? *(To Sridhar.)* So long as you sound convincing. To them.

SRIDHAR: Yes.

JITEN: So, sound convinced.

SRIDHAR: I'll have to work on it. *(Suddenly.)* You don't have very much experience in advertising, do you? *(Pause.)* I mean, you got this agency by chance, didn't you? Somebody owed you money and you took over his agency. You have other businesses. So I suggest you let professionals handle this. *(Pause.)* Why don't you want to change the campaign?

JITEN: *(snaps his fingers and points at him.)* I don't have to give you a reason.

SRIDHAR: But – this is a suicide mission.

JITEN: So go die.

SRIDHAR: *(to Nitin.)* What do you feel about this?

NITIN: *(to Jiten.)* We will discuss it tomorrow.

JITEN: What's wrong with tonight?

NITIN: When we are alone.

JITEN: So we can be alone now.

SRIDHAR: *(picks up his helmet.)* I guess I'll make a move. I'll pick up Lalitha and go home. Let you know how far they've progressed with the ball.

JITEN: Wait!

NITIN: Let him go.

JITEN: I haven't finished with him yet.

SRIDHAR: Is there anything left to be discussed?

JITEN: You think you are a smart ass, don't you? *(Pause.)*

SRIDHAR: *(with dignity.)* I think I am above average, yes.

JITEN: And you think we aren't?

SRIDHAR: I never said that.

JITEN: But you think that.

SRIDHAR: No. Never.

NITIN: Just let him go, Jitu.

JITEN: *(grins and walks to Nitin.)* I'm in the mood.

NITIN: What do you want from him?

JITEN: *(sitting on the couch.)* Do you know what this bed is for?

SRIDHAR: I beg your pardon?

JITEN: It's the biggest advantage of having an office on Grant Road. It was pointed out to me by the bugger who sold this place to me. No checking into seedy hotels in City Market. Just drive down Lavelle Road and pick one up. Bring her here and pack her off in half an hour. You save a lot of time.

SRIDHAR: If there's nothing else, I'll be on my way.

JITEN: It's a regular thing for Nitin and me. Driving out. Picking a couple up.

SRIDHAR: *(to Nitin.)* Goodnight.

JITEN: I'm talking to you, you–

SRIDHAR: What do you want from me?

JITEN: I want you to pick one up for me.

SRIDHAR: What?

JITEN: What's the matter? You haven't picked up any before?

SRIDHAR: No!

JITEN: It's time you did.

SRIDHAR: You want me to get you a whore?

JITEN: *(throws his car keys on the table.)* Here. Use the car. *(Sridhar stares at the keys.)* What are you staring at? Go on! *(Lightning outside.)*

SRIDHAR: No! *(To Nitin.)* What does he take me for?

JITEN: You call yourself an advertising professional and you don't want to pimp?

SRIDHAR: This is insane! *(To Nitin.)* Do you think this is fair? *(No response. To Jiten.)* Look, I can listen to you and carry out your orders as far as work is concerned. I may not agree on many things but professionally, you are my boss. But this… I – I've got a reputation to – I mean what if someone sees me and tells my wife? *(Pause.)* And it's starting to rain.

JITEN: *(picks up the keys.)* Good. They'll pile into the car even before you stop. *(Holds out the keys.)*

SRIDHAR: A man has his tolerance limit, you know! And this is something – me pick up a woman for you! *(Jiten doesn't move his extended arm. Sridhar is fighting tears of humiliation. He snatches the keys and rushes out.)*

JITEN: *(smirking.)* Crazy bastard. *(Picks up his drink.)*

NITIN: Jitu.

JITEN: Ya.

NITIN: Why did you say we both pick them up? *(Lightning and thunder. Baa's area is lit. She is alone.)*

BAA: Oh, it is starting to rain! The mud. Why can't I smell the mud? First rains always smell so good. Oh. It rained yesterday. It rained on my wedding day. He asked me before marrying him if I will sing! He knew that I could sing! You want me to sing only for you? *(Laughs.)* I will sing for everyone! Why are you so angry? Quickly – go away. Someone is coming! We must not see each other before the marriage, it is bad! But I saw. I saw him! He is dark! Dark! And I am so fair! My children will be dark, like him! *(Smiles.)* Two sons! I have given you two sons! The younger one is beautiful, like my father! He has my blood! Don't kiss him! You will leave tobacco on his cheek. Don't spit! Oh, the whole house smells of you! I have married such a villager! Aah! You slapped me? Never, never slap me. Nobody has hit me. The men in our family are decent. Wait, where are you taking my Jitu. Jitu, wait! Wait! *(The lights fade out on Baa. Nitin and Jiten are drinking. Jiten notices the bonsai on Nitin's table.)*

JITEN: What the shit is that?

NITIN: A plant.

JITEN: I know. But why so ugly?

NITIN: It's all art.

JITEN: And I can fart. *(Drinks.)* You want to discuss. The joker is out of the way. So discuss.

NITIN: Praful is up to something. I don't like this.

JITEN: You don't know how to handle him. He is inferior. Just keep reminding him of that.

NITIN: And you think his money is enough?

JITEN: Till we get the property.

NITIN: *(sighs.)* I don't know. Praful may be cleverer than we think he is.

JITEN: Why do you think like that?

NITIN: He made me marry his sister, didn't he? *(Pause.)* We've got to sell the property while Baa is alive.

JITEN: Will she agree?

NITIN: I can talk to her.

JITIN: Try. She will listen to you.

NITIN: Jitu. I think I should tell you something. *(Pause.)* She made me promise I wouldn't tell you. *(Pause.)*

JITEN: So tell me.

NITIN: Baa showed me her will. *(Jiten listens interestedly.)* I thought she would leave the house to me. I have always been her favourite.

JITEN: I know. It never made a difference to me.

NITIN: It was difficult for me. I had to live up to her expectations. *(Pause.)* Perhaps I have failed. *(Lightning.)* Or perhaps it's because of her. She didn't leave the house to me. She showed me a copy of the will.

JITEN: When?

NITIN: Just before the stroke.

JITEN: And you didn't tell me.

NITIN: I was too confused. Why not me? There was only one reason. She was disappointed.

JITEN: It's your wife, not you, she dislikes. What difference does it make whether you get it or I get it? It's still ours.

NITIN: She hasn't left it to you either. *(Pause.)*

JITEN: Who has she left it to? Even if it's Dolly, it's no problem.

NITIN: It's not Dolly.

JITEN: Oh. Then who?

NITIN: Daksha.

JITEN: Daksha?

NITIN: She told me. As if to apologize to me. She felt her house would be safe – in Daksha's hands. She wanted Daksha to be provided for. She felt we would all of us – would look after her better if she–

JITEN: She will have to change her will.

NITIN: She won't. She will never give it to you.

JITEN: But she will give it to you.

NITIN: No. She won't.

JITEN: I tell you she will.

NITIN: She has never forgiven me!

JITEN: Make her forgive you!

NITIN: How?

JITEN: Get rid of Alka! *(Pause. Nitin turns to Jiten.)*

NITIN: *(weakly.)* No.

JITEN: Throw her out of the house. This time, for good. Damn Praful's money! The property is more important. You want to get even with Praful? This is your chance. Say damn to his money and damn to his sister! Your marriage never worked. She is a drunkard. An alcoholic. Your wife is a boozer and you still keep her? What kind of a man are you? *(Nitin has been staring at the bonsai. He picks it up and throws it on the floor. The container breaks. Sridhar enters. He stops and looks at the bonsai. He slowly bends and picks it up.)*

(Barks out.) Where's the whore?

SRIDHAR: Outside.

JITEN: Bring her in.

NITIN: I'll wait outside.

JITEN: Nitin. *(Nitin stops.)* Tonight. When we go home. *(Nitin exits. Sridhar carefully wraps the bonsai in a piece of paper.)*

JITEN: *(snaps his fingers.)* Hurry up. *(Crosses to the toilet.)* She'd better be a good piece. Otherwise I'll take it from your salary. *(Exits to the toilet.)*

SRIDHAR: *(shouting.)* She's young and fresh! *(Under his breath.)* And she is great. I had her on the back seat. You can have my leftovers. *(Sridhar takes the plant and as he exits, the beginning of a thunderstorm can be heard. The lights fade out.)*

ACT 3

Free for All!

(The setting is the same as in Act I. Alka is lying on the sofa. Lalitha is seated and lost in thought. The thumri continues to play. After a while, the kitchen light goes off and Dolly enters from the kitchen. She stops and looks at Alka. She goes to the stereo and stops the music.)

DOLLY: Alka, wake up.

ALKA: I'm not asleep.

DOLLY: Sit up.

ALKA: Go away. It's late. Go home.

DOLLY: This is my home. Look, it's raining! Come! Come and see how wonderful it looks!

ALKA: Is it raining?

DOLLY: Yes! Come look.

ALKA: Why?

DOLLY: Because you like the rain!

ALKA: Do I?

DOLLY: Of course you do. You love getting wet and having your sari cling to you. Your bra and choli showing. And you love doing a filmi number in the rain.

ALKA: No, I don't.

DOLLY: *(laughs.)* I was just teasing you.

ALKA: *(gets up, looking a little dazed.)* I think the last drink really got – *(Notices Lalitha.)* Who are you?

LALITHA: I beg your pardon!

ALKA: *(to Dolly.)* When did she come?

DOLLY: *(looks through the window.)* There are puddles forming. *(To Alka.)* She has been with us all evening.

ALKA: All evening? You mean – we told her? She knows?

DOLLY: You told her. Anyway, what difference does it make?

LALITHA: I promise not to tell anyone.

ALKA: Oh! *(Rubs her head. To Dolly.)* I'm sorry.

DOLLY: *(enjoying the rain.)* That's okay.

ALKA: Does this – Will this make any difference to you?

DOLLY: No, silly. Why should it? It's nice to have an audience.

ALKA: *(smiles.)* An audience. *(Laughs.)* An audience! I never thought of it that way.

LALITHA: I'm sorry. I don't think I like being an audience.

ALKA: Would you prefer being a participant?

LALITHA: No! Certainly not!

ALKA: *(to Dolly.)* How much does she know?

DOLLY: She knows about Kanhaiya. That's all. So let's keep it that way.

ALKA: Of course.

DOLLY: I prefer this. The half-truth and nothing but the half-truth. *(Laughs at her own joke.)*

LALITHA: Is this some kind of a game? *(Dolly and Alka both laugh.)* Has this anything to do with–

DOLLY: A game!

LALITHA: And what about Daksha?

DOLLY: *(her smile fades.)* What about her?

LALITHA: Is she part of this – whatever it is society that you have formed?

DOLLY: What do you mean, society?

LALITHA: You know – love on the side or whatever you call it. Does Daksha also hit it off with Kanhaiya?

DOLLY: How dare you?

LALITHA: *(sarcastically.)* I'm sorry if I said something immoral. *(Alka suddenly bursts into loud laughter.)*

DOLLY: What's so funny? *(Alka continues to laugh.)* Stop it, Alka.

ALKA: Daksha – and Kanhaiya! *(Laughs.)*

DOLLY: Don't.

LALITHA: Aha! So there is something there!

ALKA: *(another wave of laughter.)* Daksha and Kanhaiya!

DOLLY: Shut up!

ALKA: That was really clever!

LALITHA: Are you people for real?

ALKA: We must be! Otherwise where did all the booze go?

DOLLY: *(to Lalitha.)* I think it's disgusting that you should talk about a fourteen-year-old like that. Especially to her mother.

LALITHA: I'm sorry. I wasn't too sure what values you'd retained and what you'd given up.

ALKA: Fourteen? I didn't know Daksha was fourteen.

DOLLY: Don't pretend.

ALKA: A very bright girl.

DOLLY: Of course!

ALKA: Learning dance and all that.

LALITHA: Look. I'm sorry, I didn't mean what I said. I'm a little tipsy too.

ALKA: But you've had nothing!

LALITHA: I've had enough, thank you. For me, that's too much. *(Alka crosses to the window.)*

DOLLY: This is the perfect weather to listen to ghazals.

ALKA: Play the thumri again.

DOLLY: Whatever you say.

ALKA: The same one. Rewind it. *(Dolly rewinds the cassette. Alka looks out of the window. Lightning.)* The old woman is outside. She's fast asleep! Even in the rain. All she has is that tarpaulin.

LALITHA: She'll be dry. It's waterproof.

ALKA: Good for her she found it. *(The thumri plays softly.)*

DOLLY: How wonderful it must be to sing like that! *(Sits down on the sofa.)*

LALITHA: *(enjoying the thumri.)* This is the first time I've heard Naina Devi.

DOLLY: Do you know Naina Devi is not her real name? She was a queen!

LALITHA: A queen! You mean – royal?

DOLLY: She married into royalty. Imagine. She could have lived her life comfortably in royal grace and become a Rajmata. But she wanted to sing! She wanted to sing songs of love. Thumris – sung in her days only by tawaifs. The queen wanted to sing love songs sung by whores! Why? Nobody knew. She'd seen a performance by a tawaif in her youth. The sound of the sarangi and ghungroos remained with her forever. She went ahead and sang! Her husband supported her. At times she was mistaken for a tawaif But it didn't matter! It didn't matter to her because she was singing! That was all that was important to her. Today, she is called the queen of thumri. *(Alka stops the music.)* Why did you do that?

ALKA: I want to play something else. *(Searches for a cassette.)*

DOLLY: First you say you want to listen to – *(Lalitha laughs suddenly.)* What's so funny?

LALITHA: Oh, nothing at all.

DOLLY: There must be something.

LALITHA: Your story. It just reminded me of a poem we learnt in school. It was in Hindi, but we all had to translate it into English as an exercise. *(Thunder.)*

ALKA: Oh! It's going to pour!

LALITHA: The poem was – let me see.

ALKA: *(interested.)* 'Jhansi ki Rani'.

LALITHA: Yes, but how did it go? *(Remembers and recites.)*

'We'd heard her praises sung so often.

So bravely fought the Rani of Jhansi

So bravely fought the manly queen…'

ALKA: 'Khoob ladi mardani woh to…' *(Lightning.)*

DOLLY: Bravely fought the manly queen?

LALITHA: Silly, isn't it? I guess it sounds better in Hindi.

DOLLY: Why manly?

ALKA: Because she was brave.

LALITHA: I always laugh when I remember that poem. I guess it just means that she was brave.

ALKA: Brave enough to qualify as a man.

LALITHA: Full of manly valour. You know – it may not be a bad idea if Dolly came as the Rani of Jhansi for the ball!

DOLLY: Me? Dressed as a brave queen?

ALKA: I would like to come dressed like that! Dolly, can I come as the queen instead of you? Please?

DOLLY: Go ahead.

ALKA: Oh good. You make a tin plate armour for me. And a sword. A cardboard sword, of course. And I will remove it and swish it about, like this – *(Demonstrates.)*

DOLLY: And we can all go – bravely fought the queen! Bravely fought the queen! *(Alka stops swishing the imaginary sword.)* Full of manly valour. *(Thunder. Dolly laughs. Lalitha giggles. Alka laughs. They all burst out laughing. A silence follows the laughter.)*

LALITHA: What would you like to come as, Dolly?

DOLLY: A tawaif. *(Lightning.)*

LALITHA: What a lovely idea! I will make a beautiful mujra outfit for you. You will look wonderful in it! *(Pause.)* And Daksha? What about her? What will she come as? *(Pause.)*

DOLLY: She can wear a splendid dance costume! All silk and brocade! And temple jewellery, lots of it! And of course bells! Dancing bells!

LALITHA: That's no good. You have to come as something you are not.

DOLLY: *(picks up the bonsai.)* What beautiful fruit.

LALITHA: Yes! So tiny! *(Alka crosses to the stereo. Dolly carefully replaces the bonsai on the coffee table.)*

ALKA: What is the raaga of the rains?

DOLLY: Megh malhaar.

ALKA: Yes. Here it is. *(Inserts a cassette.)*

LALITHA: You have such good taste in music.

DOLLY: Our mother was – tried to be a singer. When she was young. We never heard her sing. *(Thunder. The raga plays. A female vocalist. Alka smiles. Suddenly she rushes to the main door and exits.)*

LALITHA: Where has she gone? *(The music starts to build up.)*

DOLLY: I don't know. *(Suddenly realizes.)* Oh! She is actually doing it! She has gone out in the rains. *(Laughs and goes to the window. Lalitha follows her.)* Look at her! *(Calls out.)* Come back! You will ruin your sari!

LALITHA: She can't hear you.

DOLLY: She is kicking the puddles! Oh! Oh no!

LALITHA: She slipped!

DOLLY: She's covered with mud.

LALITHA: The rain will wash it off if she dances a little!

DOLLY: She is dancing! Oh, I hope the watchman's asleep!

LALITHA: Look! The old woman's woken up! She's watching her.

DOLLY: *(laughs.)* She's never seen anyone like her!

LALITHA: Oh. There's a car coming.

DOLLY: Where?

LALITHA: Can't you see the lights?

DOLLY: Yes. I – Oh, my God! Alka, come inside! It's them! Alka! Come back!

LALITHA: She can't hear you!

DOLLY: They've seen her. *(Comes away from the window.)*

LALITHA: Oh dear! What will happen now?

DOLLY: Stop that music.

LALITHA: What?

DOLLY: Stop it. Turn it off.

LALITHA: Poor Alka, maybe we should–

DOLLY: Turn the damn thing off! *(Lalitha slowly crosses to the stereo and stops it. Alka enters limping, completely wet and muddy, looking unattractive. She looks at Dolly helplessly.)*

ALKA: My heel broke. I've twisted my ankle. *(Pause.)* They've come. *(Limps to the sofa, sits down, removes her sandals and massages her ankle. Suddenly angry.)* What have I done that I should feel scared? *(Jiten enters through the main door, followed by Nitin and Sridhar. They are all slightly wet. Nitin walks to where Alka is sitting. Jiten remains where he is, staring at Alka. Lalitha moves to Sridhar.)*

LALITHA: *(to Sridhar.)* Shall we leave? *(Pause. Whispers urgently.)* Let's go, Sridhar!

SRIDHAR: We can't!

LALITHA: *(looks around.)* We must!

SRIDHAR: I've come with them. It is raining. I've left the bike in the office.

LALITHA: Oh no!

JITEN: *(still looking at Alka.)* Dolly, ask your sister to change her clothes.

ALKA: I don't want to. I'll go home and then–

NITIN: Wash your face. It's filthy.

ALKA: It's okay. I'll–

NITIN. There's mud on it.

ALKA: Oh! *(Wipes her face.)* We'll leave soon. Just give me five minutes.

NITIN: *(roughly.)* Get up! We are leaving now! (Fo*rces Alka. Alka stumbles and almost falls on the coffee table.)*

SRIDHAR: Careful! *(Makes an attempt to help her up.)*

ALKA: *(refusing his help.)* It's all right. I – I *(Hobbles to Dolly.)*

SRIDHAR: *(follows her.)* Are you sure you are all right?

DOLLY: Does it hurt?

ALKA: No. I'll be fine.

NITIN: Let's go. There's something I want to discuss with you.

ALKA: Oh. Something – serious?

NITIN: Yes.

ALKA: *(a little frightened.)* No. I – I want to be with Dolly for a while.

JITEN: Tell her now. Right here! *(Pause.)*

NITIN: Go look at yourself in the mirror.

ALKA: *(sharply.)* I know I look indecent! Ask your brother to stop staring at me!

NITIN: What did you say? *(Jiten crosses to the bar.)* Just repeat what you said.

ALKA: *(watching Jiten.)* There's no need.

DOLLY: Alka, come up.

ALKA: No!

JITEN: Ask her what she was doing outside in the rain.

ALKA: I don't know! I don't know what I was doing outside. Aren't there times when you don't know what you are doing? *(To Nitin.)* What's the harm in that? Huh? *(No response.)* Tell me. What's the harm?

NITIN: None. There's no harm in that.

ALKA: You agree with me? Don't you? *(Thunder.)* You do see what I mean? Dolly, did you hear that? You are always saying that I imply I've got a better deal. He is understanding. *(To Nitin.)* I know I haven't been an ideal housewife. And you haven't been a – well, a competent husband. But who's complaining? Nobody's perfect! *(Laughs.)* Nobody's perfect! Look at me! Saying all the wrong things. I should be thanking you for being on my side. But you know me. I was never good at flattery. Thank God you understand me. *(To Dolly.)* Dolly, I feel sorry for you. Having a lech for a husband. A saint for a brother and a lech for a husband.

JITEN: *(to Nitin.)* What more do you want? Tell her now and get it over with!

ALKA: Our saint of a brother used to warn us against men like you. *(Points to Jiten.)* And what does he do? The saint gives his sister to the sinner and disappears! *(Makes a motion of wiping her hands.)* Finished. Matter over. Or is it? The saint has another sister who is *(slaps her own face.)* bad, bad, bad. He beats her till she gets better. And he has this friend. A best friend! The sinner's brother turns out to be his best friend. Not such a coincidence.

NITIN: You are drunk!

ALKA: He called. Praful called me.

NITIN: *(to Jiten.)* We won't take it! We won't take any money from him if he is the last person on–

ALKA: *(laughs.)* You fell for that one! Dolly! Do you hear? Praful wanted to come to see us, but they wouldn't let him. He – he will come.

JITEN: All right! That's enough!

LALITHA: *(to Sridhar.)* Let's go!

JITEN: *(to Nitin.)* How can you just stand there taking all this shit? If you don't have the guts to tell her, I will.

NITIN: Not now!

JITEN: *(to Dolly.)* Your sister has crossed all boundaries of decency–

NITIN: Not now!

JITEN: There's a limit to being shameless and we both feel that–

NITIN I said not now! *(Pause.)*

JITEN *(to Nitin.)* You raised your voice at me? *(The bell rings sharply.)*

BAA: *(off.)* Nitin! *(Pause. The bell rings again. Nitin goes up and exits to Baa's room.)*

LALITHA: *(timidly.)* Perhaps if you will be kind enough to take us to an auto stand.

JITEN: *(rudely to Sridhar.)* Sit! Both of you. *(Sridhar and Lalitha sit down. Jiten is staring at Alka. Dolly stands close to Alka. Baa's area is lit. Nitin is standing by her.)*

BAA: Did you go to Praful's house?

NITIN: No.

BAA: Tell him, I want to see him.

NITIN: You hate him. You never liked him. You never wanted me to be his friend.

BAA: Tell him that I – I–

NITIN: Why do you want to see him?

BAA: His sister! Don't marry his sister, Nitin!

NITIN: Oh, it's all done. Finished! She's downstairs! We were married – Oh, what's the use?

BAA: Don't be his friend.

NITIN: I will listen to you now.

BAA: I don't want her in this house! *(Pause.)*

NITIN: Will you be happy if she – wasn't in this house?

BAA: Yes. Send her away. To the neighbour's house.

NITIN: What if I sent her back to Praful?

BAA: Tell Praful that I – want to see him.

NITIN: Baa, this is important. Will you give me the house if I send her back – for good this time?

BAA: Yes. First you have to tell me something.

NITIN: Anything! Tell me, Baa.

BAA: Do you like your father?

NITIN: He is dead, Baa.

BAA: How can you say such things? *(As if to a child.)* Nitin? Do you like your father? *(Pause.)*

NITIN: *(voice changes to a child's.)* Yes, Baa. I like him.

BAA: Go away! You are not my son! You are bad, like him! *(Again, as if to a child.)* Nitin! You don't like your father, no? He's not nice!

NITIN: *(with a heavy stutter.)* Nnn-nnn-nnn-no, Baa.

BAA: Good! You are my wonderful baby! You are my prince! *(Again as if to a child.)* Nitin. You hate your father. Tell me.

NITIN: I – I – ddddon't, I dddddon't…

BAA: There he is! He is coming! Go away! Leave us alone! *(Screaming, to Nitin.)* Tell me you hate him! He hits me! Nitin, tell me you hate him! Say it!

NITIN: *(in a normal voice.)* Yes! I hate him! *(Takes Baa protectively in his arms.)* I hate you! Go away! Leave us alone! The lights go off in Baa's area.

ALKA: What's going on?

JITEN: You should be answering that question.

ALKA: There are no goings-on over here.

JITIN: You can fool Nitin, but not me. *(Loaded with innuendo.)* So, what's going on?

DOLLY: Stop it, Jiten.

LALITHA: Please, Dolly. Could you help us go home?

ALKA: Jiten, drop them at an auto stand.

LALITHA: Yes, please. It's getting late and–

JITEN: *(to Lalitha.)* Just shut up!

SRIDHAR: That's no way to talk to a lady.

JITIN: *(to Alka.)* You are clever. You understand what's going to happen to you, don't you?

ALKA: Yes.

JITEN: Good. I want him to tell it to you.

ALKA: *(trembling, leans on Dolly for support.)* I want a drink.

JITIN: *(smiling.)* Sridhar. Fix your boss's wife a drink.

SRIDHAR: *(moves to the bar.)* What will she have?

JITIN: Rum.

SRIDHAR: With anything?

JITEN: Might as well drink it neat now.

ALKA: Yes. *(Sridhar pours out rum for her.)*

DOLLY: Shouldn't... shouldn't we inform Praful?

JITEN: In good time. It's not as if somebody has died or anything.

DOLLY: Yes. That's true!

ALKA: I – I'm feeling cold.

DOLLY: You're shivering! *(Sridhar gives Alka her drink.)*

ALKA: Thank you. *(Drinks. To Sridhar.)* We haven't really met. I have seen you at the office.

SRIDHAR: Yes.

ALKA: We weren't introduced then, but... *(Drinks.)* Please excuse me but – *(Laughs nervously.)* But I'm not always like this. Dolly, is there too much mud on me?

DOLLY: *(wipes her face.)* Just a little bit.

ALKA: *(drinks.)* Oh. This makes me warm again!

LALITHA: It's the heat going out.

ALKA: What?

LALITHA: After a while, you will feel colder.

SRIDHAR: *(goes to Lalitha.)* Please. Don't say anything now.

ALKA: *(finishes her drink.)* It – it doesn't matter. By then I will be under a warm blanket. And – and tomorrow, I can stay in bed the whole day. Dolly will look after Baa. For – for another day, I mean. Won't you, Dolly?

DOLLY: Of course.

ALKA: And then – and then I will feel much better. Should I – change before I get cold again?

DOLLY: Come with me. *(Leads Alka to the stairs.)*

ALKA: *(stops and turns.)* I guess I'd better take a little up with me. *(Moves to the bar, leaves her empty glass and picks up the bottle. Glares at Lalitha.)* Rubbish. It doesn't make me cold at all. *(Dolly helps Alka up the stairs.)* You must design a lovely costume for me, Dolly. Jari and gold and – and, don't you think I will look lovely as the queen? *(Trails off.)* Praful should see me, dressed like a queen. He will be so – happy. *(Dolly and Alka exit. Baa's area is lit.)*

BAA: What do you want from me, Nitin? I will give you whatever...

NITIN: You know what I want!

BAA: Where is Praful?

NITIN: *(annoyed.)* What do you want Praful for?

BAA: My house!

NITIN: Yes?

BAA: It is Daksha's house.

NITIN: It belongs to me! You must give it to me.

BAA: Call Praful.

NITIN: Why?

BAA: *(stuttering.)* He is – he is the ttrus–

NITIN: He is what?

BAA: Tttrustee.

NITIN: Trustee? Of what?

BAA: The house! Daksha's house!

NITIN: What are you saying?

BAA: He will look after it for Daksha.

NITIN: *(disbelievingly.)* No! You can't do that!

BAA: Nobody loves Daksha in this house.

NITIN: That's not true! Jitu loves his daughter!

BAA: I don't love Jitu

NITIN: But – Why Praful?

BAA: Daksha is four now and–

NITIN: She is fourteen now!

BAA: Look! Look at Praful playing with her. My little Daksha! How happy she is with Praful. Look! This is the first time I've seen her smile! She is smiling at Praful! She is trying to get up to go to him! Oh, Praful loves my Daksha! Praful will look after her when I'm gone!

NITIN: What have I done to deserve this? Oh God! All my life I have listened to you and obeyed you. Only once have I gone against your wishes, and you punish me for that? But he is to blame. Praful tricked me into marrying her! If you want to hate anyone, hate him. I hate him now! Do what you want with the property but don't let him run my life! He is out to get us! Alka can stay here, or go away, or drink herself to death, I don't care. It doesn't make a difference to me! But get him out of my life! *(Lighting. The light goes off in Baa's area.)*

NITIN: *(off.)* Get him out of my life!

LALITHA: What's going on?

JITEN: If you open your trap once more, you will regret it.

SRIDHAR: Be more polite! It's my wife you are talking to!

JITEN: Screw your wife!

SRIDHAR: *(getting up, violently.)* Now listen you – I've had enough!

JITEN: You want to protect your wife from whom? From me?

SRIDHAR: Just don't talk to my wife, okay?

JITEN: I wouldn't lay her even if she got me the ReVaTee account. *(Sridhar crosses to Jiten, takes his glass and throws its contents on Jiten's face. Jiten gets up and grabs Sridhar by the throat. Sridhar kicks about and beats him but is overpowered. Lalitha screams.)*

LALITHA: No! Leave him alone! *(Tries to free Sridhar in vain. Sridhar is gasping.)* Please! Leave him! Let go of him! *(Jiten lets go. Sridhar falls, gasping loudly.)*

JITEN: If you show your face in my office again, I'll kill you. *(Exits to the kitchen, wiping his face on his sleeve. Sridhar is still gasping. The kitchen light comes on.)*

LALITHA: *(helps Sridhar up.)* Oh God! Are you all right?

SRIDHAR: *(in a cracked voice.)* Stop fussing!

LALITHA: Let's get out of here. God! These women are sick!

SRIDHAR: With husbands like these, who blames them?

LALITHA: Come on!

SRIDHAR: I'm doing it. Now I'm sure. I'm walking away with the account.

LALITHA: Sshh! We'll talk about that at home. Let's get out of here. *(Sridhar staggers to the door while Lalitha picks up her things.)* Wait!

SRIDHAR: What is it?

LALITHA: The bonsai.

SRIDHAR: You want to take it back?

LALITHA: No. It hasn't been watered. It'll die!

SRIDHAR: Never mind! It's their headache. We'll have to walk to the main road and hope to get an auto.

LALITHA: I can't just let it die! What a waste of effort!

SRIDHAR: Oh, for God's sake!

LALITHA: *(moves towards the kitchen, then stops.)* Oh no. He's in there. *(Crosses to the window.)* Well, I'll just take some rain water in my hands. I'll only need to sprinkle a little. *(Stretches cupped hands outside the window. Suddenly withdraws.)* I can't believe it!

SRIDHAR: What?

LALITHA: I must be hallucinating or something!

SRIDHAR: *(moves to the window.)* What is it?

LALITHA: There's an auto parked right outside! Go! Go quickly and grab him. Run!

SRIDHAR: Yes! *(Rushes out, then stops at the door.)* If he acts smart, break the bonsai on his head! *(Exits.)*

LALITHA: *(looking out of the window.)* Oh, what's that? The auto driver! He is climbing the wall! Where's he going? To the servants' quarters! *(Spots Sridhar.)* Sridhar! Sridhar, wait! He's gone inside the – oh, what's the use? *(Collects rainwater in her cupped hands. Dolly enters from the bedroom. She has changed into her nightie. Lalitha takes some water quickly and sprinkles it on the bonsai.)*

DOLLY: What are you doing? *(Lalitha goes back to the window for more water. Dolly notices the kitchen light.)* Who's in the kitchen? *(No response.)* I asked, who is in the kitchen?

LALITHA: *(quickly sprinkling the water.)* Your Kanhaiya!

DOLLY: Stop lying and tell me who's in the kitchen?

LALITHA: Your Kanhaiya has visitors. Did you know that?

DOLLY: Have you gone mad?

LALITHA: They are probably talking about you!

DOLLY: Don't be silly.

LALITHA: You think they don't? They probably are comparing notes now and they'll laugh. It's a big joke for them.

DOLLY: What is?

LALITHA: Your – availability. Look. I sympathize, I understand, but take my advice and stay away from them. They can turn nasty anytime.

DOLLY: They who?

LALITHA: Kanhaiya and his friends! I just saw one of them!

DOLLY: Oh, stop making up things! I asked you, who's in the kitchen?

JITEN: *(enters with an ice pail, to Lalitha.)* You are still here?

LALITHA: M-my – husband has gone to get an auto.

JITEN: *(at the bar.)* Get out of my house.

LALITHA: I'm sorry but if we hadn't been asked to come, we wouldn't have.

JITEN: You're being asked to go now. So get the hell out!

DOLLY: My husband! So civilized and courteous!

JITEN: What's the matter with you? I'm not throwing you out!

DOLLY: No. You won't. You can't. *(Lightning.)*

JITEN: Want to bet?

DOLLY: You stopped Praful from coming here.

JITEN: Ya. I did that. So?

DOLLY: And you want to get Alka out.

JITEN: Maybe. *(Thunder.)*

LALITHA: Oh, it's showing no signs of stopping! *(Moves to the window.)*

DOLLY: Oh please, Jiten! Don't let your brother do that! *(Controls herself.)* No, I won't repeat myself.

JITEN: I don't care.

DOLLY: You can't throw me out because I'm leaving of my own free will. Doesn't that hurt you?

JITEN: It doesn't mean a bloody thing.

DOLLY: It doesn't mean a bloody thing! Why can't I say it?

JITEN: Say it if you want to.

DOLLY: You know I can't! You know very well I can't walk out on you! You know it, so why should I pretend you don't?

JITEN: Why pretend you can leave?

DOLLY: You win. Again.

JITEN: That's because I know what I want. You don't, so you lose.

DOLLY: When have I ever won? Once yes, once I did. When I became a mother.

JITEN: What are you getting at?

DOLLY: When I became a mother.

JITEN: Get Lalitha out of here.

DOLLY: You do remember that, don't you?

JITEN: Let her go and then we'll talk.

DOLLY: Why should I?

JITEN: What difference does it make to you if–

DOLLY: It's because she is here that I want to talk about it. Let her know!

JITEN: No!

DOLLY: Shall I wait for her husband to come as well?

JITEN: You can't!

DOLLY: What will you do to stop me?

JITEN: *(advances towards her.)* I might, I might–

DOLLY: What will you do? Kill me? Then you will have to kill Daksha as well! *(Lights on Baa and Nitin.)*

BAA: How can you say Jitu loves Daksha? How can you say that?

NITIN: How can you say that you love her?

BAA: I love her! She is my blood!

NITIN: You had denied it!

DOLLY: Go on. What are you waiting for? Strangle me.

NITIN It all happened because you denied Daksha was your blood!

DOLLY: You should have strangled me then, when Baa told you.

BAA: That was the day I got the letter. Praful was lying!

DOLLY: I know! He lied! But what a price to pay!

NITIN: So he lied. But you did far worse!

BAA: No!

JITEN: Baa provoked me. It was her fault!

BAA I did not want this. I did not know…!

DOLLY: You didn't have to listen to her! She called me a whore and you believed her?

BAA: I was angry with Praful.

NITIN: I was angry with him too, but I did not–

BAA: Praful! Where is he? I want him to say he has forgiven me!

JITEN: I was drunk then. I was angry with Praful!

DOLLY: You were angry with Praful and you hit me?

JITEN: *(almost in tears.)* That was fifteen years ago!

BAA: The house! Praful, take care of my Daksha!

NITIN: It isn't that easy.

BAA: But he lied to me!

JITEN: How do you expect me to remember what I felt then?

BAA: He is guilty also!

DOLLY: You don't have to remember. It's there in front of you! Fifteen years ago!

JITEN: I know!

DOLLY: Fifteen years ago. Hardly married for a year. Praful comes to visit us. The same day, your mother receives a letter from her cousin in Ahmedabad. What fate! It had to be the same day! And it had to be that crucial month for me! What was in that letter? Our whole history. Including the portion which Praful hadn't told you about.

BAA: Their father is not dead! Nitin, Jitu! They have lied to us!

DOLLY: I didn't know. I didn't know he had told you he was dead!

BAA: Ask him! He is there in front of you! That cheat!

NITIN: The damage is done!

DOLLY: Yes, we'd told our neighbours that. But you two were – marrying us. He should have told you the truth!

BAA: Read this letter, you liar! Your father is not dead!

DOLLY: How were we to know he hadn't?

BAA: He is alive! Living with his wife and four children!

DOLLY: My mother didn't know about his first wife till later. She was deceived too!

BAA: Your mother is a keep, a mistress! My sons have married the daughters of a whore!

DOLLY: Your mother never understood that. She blamed it on us!

BAA: Jitu. Throw him out of the house!

DOLLY: She turned her anger on us.

BAA: Jitu, throw her out as well. Whore!

DOLLY: And you hit me! Jitu, you beat me up! I was carrying Daksha and you beat me up!

BAA: No! Jitu, hit her on the face but not on the – stop it Jitu! On the face, only on the face! Enough! Stop! *(The light goes off in Baa's area.)*

DOLLY: At the hospital, you told them I fell down the stairs! Daksha was born – two months premature. With the cord around her neck! *(Pause.)* I saw her and I knew! I knew instantly! Your mother loved her more than was natural! Praful loved her. More than was natural. You love her. You love her more than Baa or Praful! Because you feel the most guilt!

JITEN: I didn't mean to – you know I didn't. It was Baa! Blame her but not me! She is my daughter! *(Crying.)* Get her back! Get her from wherever she is. I want her home.

DOLLY: *(to Lalitha.)* You want to see her dance? They teach her dance where she goes! Only they call it physiotherapy. I'll bring her tomorrow from her – special school and she will dance for you! Like this – *(She demonstrates a spastic's uncoordinated arm and neck movement with her eyes dilated. Laughs and turns around. To Jiten.)* Right, Jitu? Isn't that the way she dances? *(Repeats the movement. Jiten looks away.)* Look! Look!

JITEN: *(sobbing.)* No! No. *(Points to Baa's room.)* She made me do it! She did it!

DOLLY: No! Oh no! I will not let you get away so easily! They were your hands hitting me! Your feet kicking me! It's in your blood! It's in your blood to do bad!

JITEN: *(hysterically.)* No! I will not believe you! I refuse to believe you! *(Rushes out of the main door. Alka appears on the landing. She is in a nightie and has a blanket wrapped around her.)*

ALKA: Dolly. *(No response. Staggers to Dolly.)* I'm still shivering, Dolly. She's right. I'm getting… cold. *(Dolly suddenly embraces Alka, as if to keep her warm, and rocks her.)* Do you mind if I sleep here tonight?

DOLLY: I don't know. I don't know. *(Alka lies down on the sofa. Sridhar rushes in.)*

SRIDHAR: Somebody stop him. Stop that murderer! *(Dolly doesn't respond.)*

LALITHA: Why – what–

SRIDHAR: He's running over her! He's running the car over a beggar woman! Over and over! *(Rushes to the window.)* He's still at it! God! Stop it! Stop! *(After a while, slowly.)* He's killed her! He's – he's gone! *(Lalitha crosses to the window and looks out. Lightning. She turns away, utterly repulsed.)*

LALITHA: Oh God! What a horrible…! *(Pause.)*

SRIDHAR: *(comforting her.)* Let's get out of this hell. *(They walk towards the door. Lalitha is about to pick up her things.)*

LALITHA: Sridhar. Wait for me outside.

SRIDHAR: Why, what do you –?

LALITHA: Just do it. Please.

SRIDHAR: Don't be long. *(Exits. Lalitha circles around Dolly. Dolly is frozen.)*

LALITHA: I just want to know something. We'll probably never meet again but… I think I know the answer but – *(Takes a deep breath.)* When I told you Kanhaiya was in the kitchen, how did you know I was lying? *(Dolly doesn't respond.)* Tell me. You were so sure I was lying? How? *(No response.)* Oh! I see it all now! I understand! *(Crosses and exits to the kitchen. The kitchen light comes on. Sridhar enters.)*

SRIDHAR: What's keeping you…? *(To Dolly.)* Where's my wife? *(He notices the kitchen light and exits to the kitchen but comes back after a short time.)* What's she doing at the back door, staring into space?

DOLLY: Empty space. That's all she'll find! *(Picks up the bonsai with the fruit and slowly exits to her room. Lalitha enters. She looks at Sridhar. They embrace.)*

SRIDHAR: *(breaks away.)* Come on! We have a long walk ahead of us!

LALITHA: Has it stopped raining?

SRIDHAR: *(picks up her things.)* Yes. But the roads are flooded. *(They are at the door. Again Lalitha stops.)*

LALITHA: Wait! If Kanhaiya doesn't exist, who did the auto driver come to–

SRIDHAR: Oh, come on! *(As they exit.)* We'd better go pick up my motorbike now. Tomorrow, I'm going to the police. I want to see that animal locked up! I'm a witness to… *(Exits with Lalitha. Nitin comes slowly down the stairs. He looks at Alka, asleep on the sofa.)*

NITIN: He tricked you too, didn't he? How can you still love your brother after what he did to you… That's right. Don't answer. Just sleep. *(Laughs.)* You always were a heavy sleeper. Thank God. Those times when I used to spend the night at your place, I used to sleep on his cot. And he would sleep on a mattress on the floor, beside me… When all the lights were out, I would lie on the cot. Waiting. For at least an hour… I would get up and quietly walk to your room… Yours, your sister's and your mother's. To make sure… That's right. Don't wake up. Just sleep. And I would go back to Praful's room… and kneel… At times he would wake up immediately. At other times I would lean forward to look at him. Close enough for my breath to fall gently on his face. And he would open his eyes… I loved him too. He is… was attractive. And he responded. Oh! But how ashamed he made me feel after! He made me cry each time! That was a game he played. And I – I was caught in it… He told me to get married… How could I? And to whom? … He told me that you knew. That he had told you… about me. And that it didn't matter to you. You only wanted the security of a marriage. He… he told me everything would work out fine… But you didn't know! He tricked you! I – I am sorry. It wasn't my fault. *(Moves to her and slowly covers her face with the blanket.)* But now, you will have to sleep. You mustn't wake up, while I... while I... I mustn't keep him waiting... *(He moves towards the kitchen.)* The office is not a good idea... too many people passing by... but here – the outhouse. Perfect. Yes. Don't wake up. Stay drunk. You mustn't watch... those powerful arms... *(Exits to the kitchen. The kitchen light goes off. The thumri plays. Spotlight on Alka's huddled figure. Slow fade out.)*